MY BAD TEQUILA

Library of Congress Control Number: 2010913721 Austin, Rico.

Copyright © 2024 Rico Austin. 2nd Edition. All rights reserved.

No part of this book may be reproduced or transmitted in any form or by any means, graphic, electronic, or mechanical, including photocopying recording, or taping without the written consent of the author or publisher.

Briley & Baxter Publications | Plymouth, Massachusetts

ISBN: 978-1-961978-22-5

Book Design: Stacy Padula

MY BAD TEQUILA

PARTS OF A TRUE STORY

NARRATIVE BY RICO AUSTIN, PHD.

SONORA, MEXICO

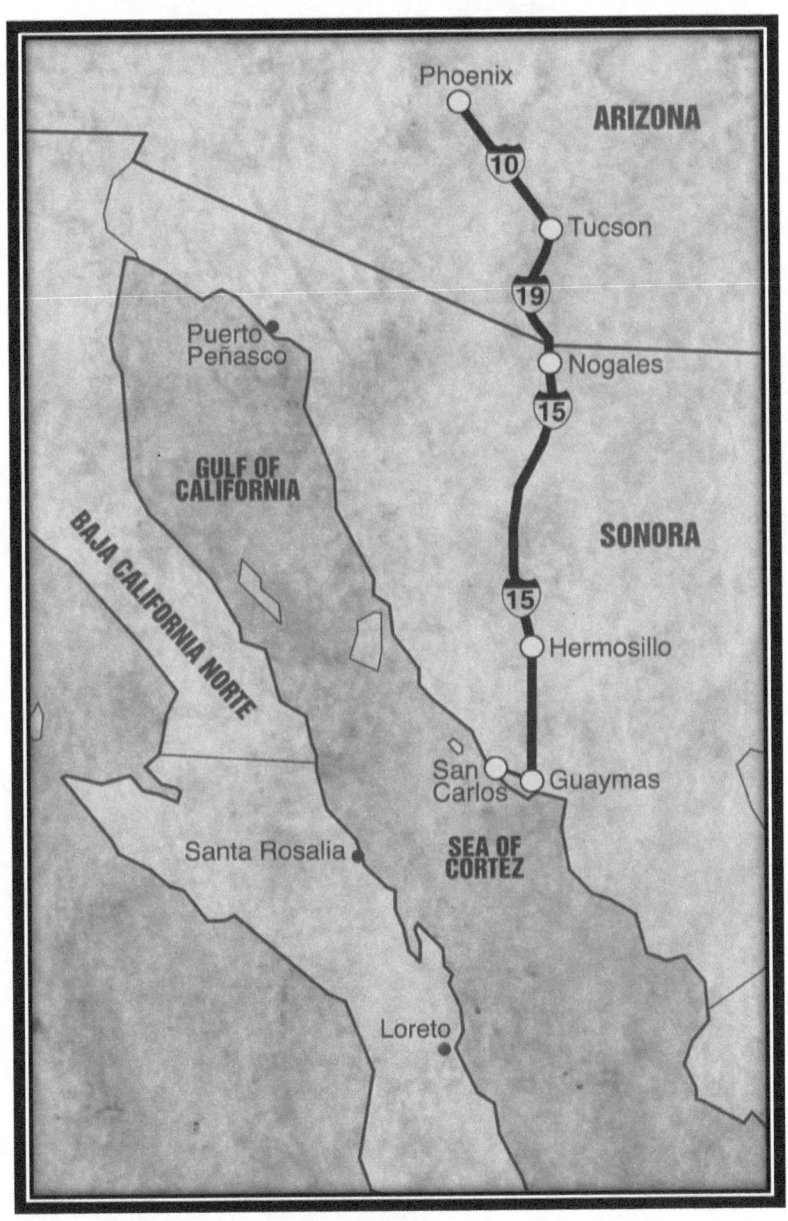

ACKNOWLEDGEMENTS

This is a revealing story sometimes I pretend is untrue. Something I wish with all my might and being it had not occurred. If only I had not worked diligently all autumn and the first part of winter to save for the cheapest vacation offered from the state of Idaho. Twenty-one years later I still see the parents awaiting the safe return of their babies, college students who had very little money but had endless dreams of a fun, exciting vacation. These young people of the "Baby Boomer Generation" who indulged in selfish pleasures, but paid their own way, by their own sweat. This generation, of which I am a part, who wanted to experience life to the fullest and did.

This is a novel concerning life, death, and the pursuit of happiness. I write from my experience and I may or may not embellish. (Please see fine print on page 4) I write what I know as did Mr. Ernest Hemingway (aka Papa) and Mr. John Steinbeck.

"In order to write about life, first you must live it," as the great Hemingway said.

Ernest Hemingway – RIP, Mr. John Grisham, John Steinbeck RIP, Jack London – RIP, Mr. Kenny Chesney, Mr. Jimmy Buffett – RIP, Mr. Toby Keith – RIP, Mr. Alan Jackson, Mr. George Strait, Mr.

Garth Brooks, Mr. Merle Haggard – RIP, Mr. Shawn Mullins, The Eagles, my hat is off to you all. Many thanks for your inspiration. I have spent hours reading your books and listening to your lyrics and music, sometimes with a drink in my hand, sometimes without.

Mr. Sammy Hagar for a chance meeting, listening to good old rock'n'roll and folk music in a small fisherman's bar. Who better knows tequila than you or me?

I wish to dedicate this book to seven-plus of my best friends and also to my family who have believed in me from my humble beginnings: Rich Collins, Matt Beckler, Patricia Beals, Rick Dancer, my dear mother Nina Austin Hayes, my now-deceased grandmother Deverl Nina Shippy Morris Eells, my deceased dad Tommie F. Austin, my wife Connie, who still puts up with my antics and stories, and, of course, all three of my younger brothers – David R.I.P., Michael and Samuel. Honorary mention to my many aunts, uncles and cousins and all my friends who I have been fortunate to have met all over the globe during my fun, simple and sometimes outrageous life including *mis amigos* in San Carlos, Mexico.

Muchas gracias to my fellow T-Birds: Kurt Pitzer, Chris Morin, Greg Clarke, Ken Adkins, Kevin Daly, and Jeff Byrd. Thank you for your assistance in editing and/or your true friendship as *amigos*.

Thank you to all my Facebook friends and the followers of the Official My Bad Tequila Fan Page, which include many helpful published and nonpublished authors from the Writers Dock Party, (you know who you are) founded by *amiga* Dr. Karen Penniman Lysik.

Thank you to Gerri Ortiz-Matz for the photograph of Tetakawi Mountain that was used for part of the novel cover.

Thank you, Artisan Colour of Scottsdale for the printing of marketing materials. Visit them at www.ArtisanColour.com.

Thank you to Elly Garrison for co-writing with me the hit single song "My Bad Tequila" inspired by this novel and sharing the same name. And to Bob, Josh, John, Bill, Bodie, Tim and Adam of the band QuarterDeck for the incredible musical sound of "My Bad Tequila."

Thank You, Josh Latham for the author's bio picture on the back cover which was shot in Portland, Oregon.

Special Thanks to my wife Connie for designing the cover and all the graphic design work involved in making the novel cover a work of art in itself and placement of the photos so perfectly.

The novel "My Bad Tequila" began on my goddaughter Paris's birthday, 12/18/2007 at 12:08 a.m. in my home in Scottsdale, AZ and was completed on my mother-in-law Janis's birthday, 6/8/2010 at 9:48 a.m. in the clouds at 34,000 feet altitude in a 737 jet plane on US Airways flight 68, originating in Phoenix, AZ.

The epic novel was signed "THE END" one hour before my arrival into Portland, OR. "My Bad Tequila" may be the first novel completed mid-air on any flight or airplane. The start dates and the ending dates were not planned or contemplated; purely coincidence or was it the subconscious mind at its finest?

Notice how the times both equal 21 and there are 21 Chapters in this novel. The address of which this novel was started equaled 21 (11874). More interesting is that I was an avid compulsive gambler of Black Jack (21) and nine months after I gave up gambling, I started writing this novel. Had I continued to gamble perhaps this story would never have made it onto paper. It is indeed a strange world in which we exist.

ENJOY the JOURNEY & "Have a Double Shot of Reality."

Special thanks to our living and deceased heroes in the Armed Forces who know that "Freedom doesn't come free."

Remembrance for those who gave their lives on that tragic day in September 2001.

"May we never forget." Dedicated on this 9th anniversary September 11, 2010.

Fine Print: This novel is a work of reality and fiction. Names, characters, businesses, organizations, places, events, and incidents are the product of 80 percent of the author's autobiography and memoirs, the other 20 percent is imagination. Any resemblance to actual persons, living or dead, events or locales is somewhat or entirely coincidental.

Some of the names may have been changed to protect the innocent, the not-so-innocent, the guilty and the inebriated.

Rico Austin

CHAPTER 1

The Bus Ride
(El Viaje Autobus)

I felt all eyes on me as I climbed onto the blue bus that had once been yellow and now sported a Porta-potty hooked up in the rear. This was the end of my Mexican Spring Break holiday, and I was headed back to the frigid March wind and perhaps a skiff of snow in Boise, Idaho.

Little did I know at that time, my life would never be the same again.

"It's all good until it turns bad," I would later remember.

"Crap, last one on," I thought to myself. My half-empty Corona with the lime trying to stay afloat dropped from my tanned, shaky hand. It didn't break as it hit the rubber mat placed strategically within the doorway to allow for such things, whether domestic or

My Bad Tequila

foreign, to bounce carelessly yet non-abrasively onto the street. The bottle rolled onto the pavement which consisted of gravel sewn together with black tar next to a partially eaten tamale covered with green salsa that was a bit too ripe. I went after my beer and picked it up, now three quarters empty as some people would say. I saw it as one quarter full. My positive outlook on life helps me see things this way.

I boarded the bus, having a bit of difficulty due to the metal support brace on my right knee. I looked at my "*amigos*," a word we used loosely, I had learned on this trip – because each person, place or thing that we encountered was our *amigo* (friend).

"Sorry for being the last person."

It was 8:12 a.m. We were supposed to be gone and on the broken asphalt highway back to life as we knew it at no later than eight a.m. There was a silence I have never heard before or since. With my thumb I trapped a bee that had been swarming around my beer, either attracted to the fruit inside the bottle or the rotten salsa smeared on the outside.

"Still nothing from Tina?" The words came slurred from my dry, swollen, partly scabbed lips, which had enjoyed too much sun and salty margaritas.

My question was answered by the anguished looks of my fellow Spring Breakers. Tina had not surfaced. The last time any of us, including her two roommates, had seen her was 36 hours earlier.

This is "My Bad Tequila." This spring getaway was supposed to be a fun experience and a pleasant memory. It ended up being more than a memory; it was an unpleasant walk through life.

We were 19 students, 3 parents and 1 scuba diving instructor named Craig on break from Boise State University. The first time I met Craig in February at the pre-trip meeting, I knew we were never going to be close.

"Let's see, Rhet Austen, that name sounds familiar," he said. Oh yes, I remember, you're the football player." Craig also served as our bus driver for the 27-hour ride, not including the night we spent in Nogales, Arizona on the grass median inside a circular, dusty, motel driveway in sleeping bags. This was the classic economy Spring Break getaway: $230 including roundtrip bus fare, five nights in a marina-view accommodation, and a welcome shot of tequila upon arrival. Each of us was excited about escaping the March cold and our studies at Boise State University and heading south to the sea, sun, and Mexican *cervezas* (beer). Most of us would have gone to the Oregon beach, though the water would have been devastatingly cold, just to put distance between us and the 29 degree Boise weather that wintry morning. The majority of travelers were scuba divers or snorkelers looking to visit the Sea of Cortez, which Cousteau called the "World's Aquarium."

This was a time before the internet. Why do I mention the internet?

Most of us, including *moi*, did not know where exactly we were headed. I had never heard of the Sea of Cortez, although I did remember learning something about a Spanish Conquistador named Cortez so I figured it was a large body of water named after him. I hadn't even taken the time to check out a book on Mexico, on San Carlos, or the Sea of Cortez. My trusting personality had taken Craig on his word that it would be the best vacation I would ever take. Craig had been there several times. I had asked him exactly how many times and his answer was always "several."

Surely some students must have taken the time to research what were to be their new surroundings, especially those who had daddy or mommy kicking moolah into the Spring Break kitty. It was probably a precursor for the student to show her or his parents the peaceful and tranquil setting where they would explore and learn about a new culture. HA!

Not me. I had told only one friend and no relatives of my plans. My mother has always made it her business to worry, whether or not there was anything to even worry about. If I told any of my relatives, be it brother, cousin, aunt, uncle or great, great uncle, my plans would always get back to the maternal person of our family – my mom. Not a relative that was even a far branch or root on our family tree knew I

My Bad Tequila

had any inclination of going to Mexico.

The thing I remember most of Craig's little presentation on San Carlos was that the weather was warm down there all year long. One word had sold me: "warm."

I wanted to get out of the cold and far from Boise, as my girlfriend and I had broken up a few weeks earlier. I was already in another relationship and needed to think hard and long about where things were headed and if it was in the right direction. It would do me good to get away, to smell Mexico or the sea. It didn't matter, though I was looking forward to some deep sea angling. I've always considered myself quite a fisherman even though it seems I have to barf each time I leave land behind.

The thought of fishing and/or getting sick reminded me of my first fishing trip back in the mid Sixties. I lost my first tooth while fishing with my dad and grandfather in Idaho up near New Meadows, at a place called Lost Lake. It was early morning, 5:30 a.m., and I was eager to have breakfast of baloney sandwiches with my two elders. I bit into the soft white bread, enveloped on the outside of one huge slab of meat a five-year-old had no business encountering. As I bit into the manwich I felt a quick jab of pain, then blood gushed from my mouth until the white bread looked as if covered with catsup. My tooth that I had been working on so gently for five days was on the wooden floor somewhere in my grandpa's 14-foot boat with an eight hp Johnson outboard motor. My dad and grandpa each gave a chuckle after discovering what had happened, and dad found an old rag for me to clean up with and made a makeshift bed at the bow of the boat. I slept for a couple of hours and when finally awoken, took a pole with a Zebco reel in my hands and caught 12 large rainbow trout that day. My grandpa told me that was my lucky tooth and I was satisfied. But, I did trade it in for money, a deal I made with the tooth fairy that night when I put it under the towel I used as a pillow. One tooth was worth one dime or a nickel depending on if there was any spare change in the house at the time.

My first IOU was from the tooth fairy, which was better than

Santa Claus had done. That prick missed our house two years in a row, just so happened to be the same two years my dad left us, not returning home after getting his weekly paycheck. We never found out what happened, but a couple of years later he reappeared and made up with my mother. Of course he had his five boys as soon as we saw his truck pull up to our trailer. This disappearing act happened several more times as we grew up, but I never got used to it. We would all wait for him to come home on payday in hopes of going to A&W or the Red Steer for cherry cokes. Four drinks would be ordered, Dad getting his own drink, and the three remaining shared among us five boys and Mom, each of us receiving half a soda. Those were some of the greatest moments of my childhood. My dad was an alcoholic and a father of five by the time he was 25 so I never blamed him. Hell, my dad was still a kid himself at the time. Mom was always the steadfast one, mean as a polecat, but I guess she had to be strict in order to keep us in line.

Even though my lucky tooth was gone, my good luck as a fisherman stayed with me throughout my years.

It was a long journey from Boise to San Carlos. The first leg of the trip was non-stop to the other side of Las Vegas, to a casino outside Boulder known as State Line. It was early morning when the bus pulled into the parking lot. Students raced off to use a regular sanitized restroom and get something to eat from the cafeteria.

We had 30 minutes reprieve from the grueling bus ride and I wanted to make the most of them. I headed straight for the casino floor and found a $2 blackjack table. I had saved $200 for spending money, which was not nearly enough for the vacation plans stored in my head. I needed and wanted more money—a lot more. But my luck in the past with blackjack had been sporadic.

Once, two years before this trip, my cousin and I went to Jackpot, NV and I lost $300, which was every last nickel I had. Luckily, Tommie had already filled his car's gas tank and we had a ride back to Boise. I did take out two lovely green felt blackjack tables and seven stools before getting roughly escorted out through a maze of hallways with rooms at every turn filled with old slot machines, roulette tables, poker tables and of course, old, used black jack tables that had been treated in the same nasty way I had abused them. As I was being physically maneuvered towards the rear of the building, I would occasionally get a fist to the midsection or face. What was at first three security guards at the scene had doubled to six. Later, I figured out that rarely does a casino guard get the opportunity to beat on a defenseless guest that had turned idiot by doing something he should have thought longer about. Just reasoning two seconds longer probably would have made the difference in choice that my actions would have taken.

Finally, a large door was pushed open and we were all outside the casino somewhere in the back near the trash dumpsters. I was thrown hard to the ground and felt two different boots kicking me in the ribs since I was protecting my head and face with arms and hands. The boots came with owners of voices angrily shouting, "Don't ever come back here again," and then, just like that I was left alone, bruised all over and bleeding from my nose and an elbow that had hit the asphalt lot at full impact. I managed to stand, brush myself off, and start walking in one direction to try and get around this massive building toward the front entrance and parking lot where my first cousin and I had left his car. I found the car, but didn't see my cousin, so I cautiously made my way across the highway to another smaller casino which I entered as discreetly as possible. I found my way to the restroom to clean my wounds and then back to wait for my Mom's sister's son to meet me at the car. I was still in disbelief over what had just occurred. This wasn't Las Vegas in the fifties or sixties; this was Jackpot, Nevada in the mid-eighties. I wasn't aware that persons not reasoning correctly were shown the ways of their wrongdoings by paid casino thugs posing as helpful security guards with a badge, billy club, and gun.

The movies portrayed this type of behavior with scenes of the "innocent" guy getting roughed up time and time again. I learned at that moment screenwriters pencil these incidents into their movies for one reason: THIS SHIT REALLY HAPPENS!!

There was also the time, too, years after my Spring Break trip:

while moving to the Phoenix, AZ area, my car broke a fan belt in Ely, Nevada and I was forced to spend the night in Hotel Nevada. I had $20 set aside for gambling that night. I took the $20 bill to the cashier and asked for two rolls of nickels as I wanted to make my *dinero* (money) last as long as possible. I then went to the only blackjack table in the town of Ely with $16 cash and two rolls of nickels and laid down my $5 bet. I won the first hand, the second hand, and the third hand, each time doubling up my bet, thanks to advice given me by the young full-breasted dealer. I drank milk and made easy decisions all night while the two hottest girls in Ely traded shifts dealing blackjack to me. (I repeat, they were the hottest girls in Ely except for a couple of gals at the Green Lantern).

By seven a.m. the next morning I had over $5500 worth of chips on the table and the girls had over $700 worth of chips in tips. I never even pulled back the covers of the bed in my room for which I had paid $39 to stay. The next morning my Ford Granada was repaired, ready and waiting at the local mechanic shop. When I was about to leave to retrieve my car, the owner of the Hotel Nevada showed up, heard the dismal news (for him) about my winnings, and offered me two free nights in Ely with all the food and drinks I wanted. He also volunteered to be my personal blackjack dealer. Lucky for me, I had a job waiting in Mesa, Arizona and a deadline to meet.

This is how it was with blackjack and me. These were the two spectrums I was accustomed to when playing, either all in or all out. Unfortunately, there was never an in-between.

Reaching the blackjack table at the State Line Casino I reached into my pocket trembling as I pulled the $200 from my money clip. I counted it slowly, then gave the dealer five of my twenties. The middle-aged female dealer counted out the hundred dollars and gave me a stack of red $5 chips. I pushed the chips back to her before she could send the $100 to the black box with the open slit and said, with the most confidence I could muster, "Money plays." The dealer glanced up at me and said, "Are you sure?" as she raked the chips in. She bellowed out, "Money plays a hundred," and dealt. She had a jack showing and

My Bad Tequila

I had an eight in the hole with a seven showing. I instantly got that same sick feeling I had in Jackpot a couple of years earlier but had no choice other than to hit. The dealer flipped me over a two; now I had 17 against possibly the dealer's 20. I hesitated and waved my hand over my cards, second guessing myself all the while. The dealer flipped her down card and it was a 5, she took another card – King, Bust.

"Yes," I exclaimed and pumped my fist into the air. The dealer put four $25 chips in front of me. I grabbed my cash and put the five twenties back with their brothers into the clip, then back into the safe refuge of my Levis. I was about to pick up the $100 worth of green chips I had just won to trade for cash.

I must have pissed off the dealer with my over exuberance. She was now my enemy, as I could tell by the tone of her voice.

"Well young man what are you going to do now, leave with all your money while you're on a streak?" She posed it as a question, yet it seemed also to me a dare.

I thought to myself, I'll get her flustered and pissed off at me and in return I'll have karma on my side of the table, so I responded, "Yeah, let's go ahead and play another hand." I added, "After all, my kid Sparky is probably still sleeping in the car."

The dealer looked at me hard. "Is your son in the car alone?"

"Of course he is, Sparky's now four years old," I retorted. "He knows to look both ways before crossing the highway." (Little did I know at that time Sparky was a role model and mascot for every student that went to or had attended Arizona State University). This sent the motherly dealer into a rage. I pushed my chips into play and blurted out, "Deal em."

And she did, hitting me with a king, nine for the house. The next card she flipped over was an ace for me and before she could give herself a card I flipped the king and shouted, "Blackjack Baby, pay me." Just like that I raked up my chips and headed to the cashier's cage with an additional $250.

I chuckled to myself, "I am going to have a great Spring Break," as I made room for $450 in my shiny money clip.

8

I used the bathroom, grabbed a turkey sandwich and walked past the blackjack table once more, giving the gal another chance to tell me, "You're not fit to be a parent and I hope you lose the rights to your child."

I climbed back on the bus, no longer feeling tired and haggard. San Carlos is approximately four-and-a-half to five hours south of the Nogales, Arizona border. After you cross the border it's a scenic drive for the first two hours, and after that sagebrush, cactus, several PEMEX gas stations and occasional huts or makeshift shanties claiming to *vende llantas* (sell tires) as a way to get lonesome truckers to stop for an inexpensive meal. Actually, I wouldn't even call them huts; shanty is the more appropriate description of the structures made from old boards, some scrap aluminum, maybe an old tire or two and any other bits or pieces found at a dump site or thrown on the side of the highway. Those homes hold poorer Mexicans and are cold in the winter and extremely hot in the summer. They leak when it rains, and it rains a lot. That broken asphalt highway known as Ruta 15 (route 15) starts in Nogales, continues through Hermosillo and then to Guaymas, which is the first place from the highway where travelers can view the sea. Highway 15 then continues down the coast to Mazatlán and beyond. We pulled into Nogales, Arizona late afternoon; we, the vacationing breakers, had been told that just across the border was a different Nogales. One called Nogales, Mexico.

After the long bus ride from Vegas to Phoenix to Tucson, past Green Valley to Rio Rico and then onto Nogales, I was ready to explore, but kept it to myself.

Each of us bedded down onto our "made-to-fit lounges." I made my bed roll out as "John Wayne" had done a hundred times and more in his Hollywood Picture career. I slipped out of my sneakers but kept the rest of my clothing in place and crawled into a green bag lined with blue which had yellow and pink strings appearing from the top or bottom depending upon where I was positioned.

I lay in my bag beside people—or "students"—that I had met earlier, three states and nearly one country away. Looking up at that

My Bad Tequila

incredible dark, clear, star-filled border sky I knew I had to go into Mexico for the evening. I could not sleep with the anticipation of vacation and what lie ahead.

Struggling to be snuggling into a deep sleep, I lay awake listening intently for another snore or heavy breathing within the park. After hearing several deep sighs and snores I decided it was time for my exit.

I slid out of my "park ranger-certified" bag, hoping all the time that no heavy crinkling sound was made available. Safely out of the bedding that had saved so many lives in Nepal, I grabbed my sneakers, put on my Boise State University ball cap and snuck across the wet grass staying deep in the shadows.

I used to be a world-class amateur (only the fact that I didn't get paid kept me from being considered a professional) at slipping out into the night when growing up. I shared a bedroom with my two youngest brothers at the far end of the trailer from my mother. Her bedroom was located at the other end of the entire length of a sixty-foot trailer. My other two brothers shared a room just on the other side of the kitchen and living room and they kept their door closed. There was no alarm or alarm code to worry about and my younger brothers slept heavily throughout the entire night. My mother was a light sleeper, but I could slip outside in the same way a ninja warrior happens upon his prey.

Having cleared the park, I opted for the partially lit sidewalk just off International Road, which led to the border.

As I walked along the sidewalk to "Mexico," the sounds and smells drew me closer. This was an experience a small northwestern boy never believed would happen or even dreamed of happening.

"In a foreign country," I thought to myself as I nonchalantly proceeded across the border after my short fifteen minute walk. Once again my heart started pumping overtime again, the same way it had been churning blood rapidly when I had arrived, played, and left the blackjack table in Vegas.

As I approached, Mexican music with accordions, mandolins

and violins filled my ears. I felt every bone and fiber in my being persuading me to dance.

I came upon the border , stayed with the sidewalk, and presto, just like that I was in Mexico.

Neon signs alit in every dark corner. "How could that be," I thought to myself as I slowed my steps into town to give myself time to take it all in.

Music was alive in the street, *hombres* (men) sitting at the taco stand, which was ready to collapse at the next major rainfall. It was glorious, yet not glorious.

Bars and hotels were all stacked against one another, with no space in between the different painted shops and entryways or doors. At the first drinking establishment I approached, a pretty young Mexican girl offered me a welcome shot of tequila. Without missing a beat, I did the shot, handed the cracked shot glass back and continued exploring this lively border town.

I was so fortunate to be coming from the United States into this country that had been instilled upon the old beliefs that you and I still hold true of the "Old West." If you had a fast gun and a fast horse your chances of survival were greatly increased. Visions that Davey Crockett, Jim Bowie, and Pancho Villa believed to be true. Yet country politics and land had put Pancho at odds with Davey & Jim. Instead of fighting one another, they should have all been great friends. Some things will never make sense.

Next thing I saw was a "Billiards *Abierto*" (Open) sign, which I guessed, meant a person could play pool if they wished to do so.

I walked pass this establishment to the next. The concrete walkway beneath me changed with every step that I took; never level, but not so uneven that a stumble took place.

Music blared throughout this mangy neighborhood, and I asked myself, "Why didn't you just choose to rest underneath those clear Arizona skies?"

My question was instantly answered as I neared the next place open for business during the dark hours of the night. Standing there

My Bad Tequila

was a long-legged Mexican gal just outside the casino. Casino and Mexico just do not seem to mix, although they do rhyme quite well. The lady motioned to me as if to say, "Come to my corner of the world." I answered her call and was immediately by her side.

She asked me in almost perfect English if I wished to have a beer inside. Who could resist? Of course I wished to have a beer inside—or outside.

My head had started to get light and my mind began to circle and play games with my psyche.

As Dr. Suess would have said if he had been writing books for alcoholics instead of small children,

"I would have a beer, a beer I would have;

This beer or that beer, any beer I would have, any beer would do;

I can drink a beer inside, I can drink a beer outside, and I can drink a beer with a bitch by my side; I can drink a beer with a can, I can drink a beer, I think I can, I can; I can drink a beer in a bottle, I can drink a beer with a model;

I can drink a beer with a cat, I can drink a beer with a rat, I can drink a beer in a hat, I can drink a beer with a rat looking at a cat in a hat;

I can drink a beer here, I can drink a beer there, I can drink a beer anywhere; if there is a beer there, if there is a beer here, I guarantee when I leave, there will not be beer anywhere."

The goldfish in the bowl looked at me as if I were crazy.

I entered the dim room just off the main drag. A jukebox stood in the one corner; in the other was a makeshift bar tended by an elderly woman who stood patiently behind it.

Alberto's Place was not full; however, there were beings milling about. I walked up to the bar with the woman I had just met, It was really nothing more than a wood plank balanced over two concrete pillars that were poorly made. The walls looked as if they were begging for just the slightest of earthquakes to rid them of their misery. I don't know how I knew this, but I did: The walls wanted to crumble and go back to their beginnings as concrete dust.

As I followed my new friend to the bar we passed a couple of slot machines and a poker table with four *hombres* playing. I stopped briefly to watch the dealer throw playing cards like Frisbees, each one landing perfectly before the person it was intended for, and each face down.

When I reached the bar she was ordering herself a double vodka, straight up. "Strange," I thought, "We are not in Russia or one of the Baltic States like Lithuania. Why would a native order something other than tequila or a Mexican beer?" I then ordered a beer not knowing what the brands were.

I was a virgin in the ways of Mexican beers.

I slowly gathered in my change from the $20 I had given the bartender, this after paying double what I would have paid in the U.S. for the same amount of alcohol. One double shot of house Vodka and a beer. The total came to $7, an astronomical amount in the mid-1980s, and I had to shake my head in disbelief. And I hadn't even left a tip. At this rate my money would not last long.

The bartender set a Tecate beer in front of me with what appeared to be a clean six-ounce glass. Normally I just drink from the bottle, but not wanting to appear unsophisticated in front of my newfound *amiga* (female friend), I poured some beer into the small glass and took a quick gulp.

I then excused myself to use the *baño* (bathroom). As I headed for the head, I spotted the centerpiece of the floor and business. It was a mosaic of two roosters fighting each other, rendered in brightly colored tile pieces. It was quite graphic, with blood splattering out in the open air as one of the roosters slashed the other with his sharp talons, or razors attached to his talons. I believe the correct lingo for this sort of action is "cockfighting."

Inside the small bathroom was one urinal, about three feet long, and engineered in such a way that several men at a time could piss. There was also a pint-sized stall for taking care of other business; it had no door. Lying just inside the stall was a semi-large piece of plywood. Being the only one in the *baño*, I unzipped my Levis and proceeded to take a leak. When I was about halfway finished, an old Mexican man came in using his damaged, worn hands as a throttle to move his ancient wheelchair. A half leg was missing on his left side and his jeans were tied in a knot to keep them from dragging or getting caught in a spoke from his moving chair. He went to the opposite end of the urinal, got my attention and then said to me, "*Cuidado, Cuidado.*" I looked at him, puzzled.

He turned his wheelchair 90 degrees and without saying another word, pulled up to the stall and proceeded to crawl from his home on wheels onto the toilet seat without touching the filthy floor. He then grabbed the piece of plywood and a makeshift shield of privacy was installed.

I finished up, zipped, buttoned and tried to wash my hands. I tried both handles, turning them completely on and then off, once again trying the same routine. Nothing. There was no water and no towels.

As soon as I returned to the bar my new woman friend asked me my name.

"Rhet. And yours?"

She introduced herself as Antonia and then added, "Do you like me?"

"Yes," I responded immediately, still thinking about what the old man had said to me and also pondering what unfortunate event had caused him to lose a leg somewhere about the knee joint.

A couple of minutes later, I saw the old man roll back into the room and to a table in a corner, only him and one other wooden chair. It looked as if he were sharing a drink with a memory or a ghost of a fallen comrade, years earlier during a happier time, before being sentenced to life in a chair.

"What does *cuidado* mean?" I asked her.

Antonia answered without giving it any thought. "It means to be careful."

I said, "Oh," wondering why the old man had chosen those

particular words when addressing me.

She then questioned me as to why I had asked, "Why? Was there a sign in the bathroom or on the floor?"

I pointed toward the old man sitting alone at a small wooden table with his wheelchair pulled up to it. "That man said, '*Cuidado, Cuidado*,' to me when I was in there."

Instantly, she shot an evil look in the old man's direction. As she did so, she turned her head slightly and that is when I spotted the Adam's apple of Antonia. Now looking closer at "her" I could see even more manly traits in "his or her" face. I grabbed my glass, took one more gulp of beer, and quickly picked up the bottle that still had more than half its original contents within. This was truly a Double Shot of Reality!

I walked as straight as I could over to the angel of an old man, setting down the beer bottle on his table. I then took off my nearly new, bright orange BSU cap and motioned that both beer and hat were for him, at the same time repeating, "*Gracias, gracias,* gracias" (thank you).

Out of the bar, I headed as fast as I could with a knee brace slowing me down, back to the safe side of the border. Before I reached the States, my head was swirling and my balance impeded, and I knew that Antonia with an O for Antonio had slipped me a "mickey." I also knew that the first shot I had tossed back had also been laced. The agent at the border asked to see my ID, which I clumsily fumbled for and luckily found then offered to the agent. He waved me across and I replaced my wallet back in my hip pocket.

I made it back to the park without any further incident other than some major staggering. I was not the same stalking ninja that had left a mere 40 minutes or so earlier. I might as well have had a cow bell around my neck. But if anyone saw or heard me climbing back into my bag it was not mentioned the next day.

I slept a deep sleep that night and was one of the last ones to rouse from my bed on the ground. As I literally crawled out of my bag of a bed, my head was throbbing horribly, but I am not one to carry aspirin as I rarely have a headache. I somberly climbed aboard the bus for the final leg of our journey. Everyone else was as chipper as a blue jay when a cloudy, rainy day finally gives way to the sun and friendlier skies.

That morning on the bus, one of my traveling companions put in a tape that included the song, "Funky Cold Medina." I could have sworn everyone was looking right at me when the lyrics were sung, "Sheena was a man." I don't know if it was just my paranoia or if someone had seen me with the "She Man."

But be assured of this, I made sure everyone heard me sing along with this phrase, "I don't want no Oscar Meyer Weiner."

Hotel Nevada in Ely, Nevada

Rico fishing trrip with his Grandpa and Dad at Lost Lake, Idaho
Where he lost his first tooth

My Bad Tequila

CHAPTER 2

The Party
(La Fiesta)

Why had I insisted that we leave our safe drunken haven at our hotel that night to party with the upper class, the pretty people who could afford Club Med? This question tormented me, even though it had only been hours since any of us had seen Tina, the energetic 20-year-old junior from Yakima, Washington. Tina was a bit wild, yet she still had an innocence about her that drew men, young and old, to her side. I felt responsible since I was the one to flag down the pickup truck for a ride. That is how she had been introduced to the three young Mexican *hombres* she was last seen with, according to my recollection.

The party was a riot, each of us instructed by Craig to dress wildly if we wanted to be named the annual "Boise State Party Person of the Year" and win a bottle of 100% agave Tequila. It was an honor that would not be forgotten once the Spring Breakers headed home. I took first place that night by wearing a white jock strap I had packed in my duffle bag, though I wasn't sure why I had chosen to pack this protective wear. It went perfectly with the smiley face painted on my buttocks. A couple of the girls I had met on the long bus ride suggested drawing on my bare ass with lipstick, liner, and other makeup crammed in their suitcase-sized purses.

Craig and two of the chaperones were the judges for our dress up or dress down party. Even though Craig had already shown he was judgmental towards me when I signed up for this getaway, he liked my ingenuity and the originality of my getup. In his late thirties or early forties, Craig had dark hair that was thinning badly. He also had an ego only scuba instructors can have. He was in good, but not great, physical shape. He came across as God's gift to young women, especially those on this Spring Break. I could tell he was already making a couple of them feel uncomfortable with his close contact and flirting. I had made up my mind just before the trip I would not hold any ill feelings or a grudge towards Craig for comments made at our first encounter. I wanted to have fun and nothing more.

I think it was about 5:30 p.m. PST; San Carlos is the same as Arizona, which does not recognize Daylight Saving Time. My costume was nothing more than a white piece of cloth. Luckily for my good physique this costume did not look bad from the front (even though I had lost a few pounds of muscle due to my surgery). The back I have no idea what it looked like, all I know is that I was a hit. What could go wrong? As I sipped on tequila hidden within a margarita I wondered where we should go next. I don't like to wear out the furniture.

As my old man used to say: "Stay too long and you start to smell, like fish."

Jumping from my folding chair that was close to its last fold, I yelled, "Let's get the heck out of Dodge."

What can I say, I'm a country boy.

I left the party, which was in Craig's large, whitewashed brick room with two single beds, a large worn chest of drawers standing about five feet high, and a cracked dirty brown washbasin. There was a bottle opener attached to the wall with a concrete nail where there should have been a soap dispenser. Just before the sink was a narrow wooden door that looked as if termites were having a love fest in the *palo verde* (green skin). This door was the entry to the odor-drenched bathroom where used toilet paper had to be put in the little green plastic trash basket lined with an OXXO bag. OXXO is the Mexican version of a bright neon-lit Circle K or 7-11 store in the good ol' US of A. Each and every bathroom I visited in Mexico on that trip had the same shit-induced smell coming from the trash as it was a big no-no to flush any TP down the commode because the sewer emptied into the Sea of Cortez somewhere down the pipeline.

 Lifting my key, I had tied onto an old lace from a tennis shoe off my neck and over my head I slid it into the keyhole and turned the knob. My room was nearly identical to Craig's except there were four single beds and a short nightstand with all the knobs missing. I had three roommates, all of whom I had met at the beginning of our trip in the Boise State University parking lot. They were all seniors and scuba butt buddies at BSU. I was lone man out. I grabbed the rusty bar at the head of the cot and dragged my bed with its bright orange and red Indian blanket to the back corner of the room. I started scratching myself even before crawling under the covers or touching the blanket, made of densely woven horsehair, much later that evening.

 Each room had a back door that led out to a small patio about four feet wide by about twelve feet in length that was enclosed by more of the whitewashed brick about twenty-four inches high. Only a two-foot wall separated us from the adjoining patio, so there was no privacy to speak of. Our patio had three old wooden chairs and no table, just an old Folgers coffee can for an ashtray.

 The hotel was a single story and laid out horizontally with each room attached to the next. There were 13 rooms, each almost identical except for the number of beds stashed in the different abodes. The first room was a makeshift office with an old scratched up bar counter in the front supporting a telephone and a worn yellow curtain drawn behind it to separate the office clerk's living quarters. The clerk behind the counter was named Luis, and as the week progressed, I learned he had three small children and a wife all sharing that tiny living space. The hotel was set upon a craggy hillside splattered with saguaro cacti, red and orange bougainvillea and the occasional *palo verde* tree. Off our balconies we could see the old marina of San Carlos with boats of every make, size, and kind. There were sailboats, high-dollar charter fishing boats, pangas, Gary's dive boats, and pleasure boats for fishing or waterskiing.

There are two marinas in San Carlos now, but at the time there was only the San Carlos marina. The Nueva Marina was built several years later on the other side of Tetakawi Mountain. Tetakawi looks like two upside down goat teats, which is where its name originates. In Spanish it is "*Tetra de la cabra*" and in the Yaqui Indian language it is "Tetakawi," which basically is "Teat of the goat" in English. Tetakawi was once the sacred landmark of San Carlos but now due to the price of ocean view and marina view property, Tetakawi is sprinkled with home sites and multimillion dollar completed homes. The Yaqui people were said to have been skillful warriors who were also good farmers and fishermen. They were quite tall in stature, but all I could think was, "they sure know how to name a mountain."

I stumbled outside and leaned against the Suburban of one of the "persons that are supposed to being looking out for you." There was one other chaperone who had left two days earlier than us with his student daughter and another coed friend. They had arrived in style and were already telling us stories about San Carlos as if they had been ahead of us by three weeks. Story was that the girl's dad had made the comment, "Like hell I'm going to let you go to Mexico alone, and there's no way in hell I'm going to ride a bus all the way to Mexico," and thus the Suburban.

Feeling the lone coyote syndrome, I walked around the complex until I could spot the sea below and thought about the party I had just left. I was feeling a slight bit embarrassed now that it was over and was beginning to realize just how ridiculous I must have

My Bad Tequila

looked. What was I thinking? Wearing only a jock strap and makeup on my butt? Must have been the lingering effect of the "mickey" the transvestite had dropped into my drink. I had been fairly quiet the last leg of the bus ride, sitting alone, looking out the window, trying to sleep. But as soon as we hit San Carlos and bought our beer and tequila I drank nonstop, trying to rid myself of the constant throb near my temple.

"What difference does it matter?" I reasoned among me, myself and I. Having fun was my goal and that is what I was doing. I shook off the guilt almost as quickly as it had come over me. It didn't matter, I could do whatever I pleased as there was only one individual that I knew or recognized from Boise State, not counting Craig the money taker and host of our excursion. I was thinking so intently that I probably stammered it aloud.

Even now, my drink was still in my hand; I gulped the margarita, licked the salt on the rim, wiped my mouth, and limped toward my room.

CHAPTER 3

Football Memoirs Part 1
(Futbol Americanos Biografia, Parte 1)

My door to the room was still open and I hobbled back in. "Geez this fucking knee is killing me," I slurred under my breath. "Not enough tequila in the country of Mexico to make this pain go away."

My mind drifted back to BSU and the next-to-the-last game of the year against the University of California Davis (or, as they like to call themselves, UC Davis). It was the last time I would celebrate victory with my teammates as a Bronco. I had worked out all season and was defensive head of the scout team. Next year I would be starting on the special teams, perhaps getting in a play-per-defensive possession. Things had been going well. The head coach had doubts about me during the summer double day workouts, but now was warming up to me.

My Bad Tequila

The defensive back coach had been my friend and mentor. Coach Mass was consistent, persistent, and had a good sense of humor. But the last time he had spoken to me in the trainer's room was not friendly. One of the many times that he made me feel at home was a Thursday night before a home game.

A little background here for those of you who are thinking of pursuing a professional career or just wanting to get a college education by playing football. Even though we were not in an actual game-playing situation we still were advised strongly to live by the rules: "Thursday through Saturday, aka game day, no alcohol. You always represent the team."

But it was Thursday evening when a bunch of us on the squad had gone downtown Boise to let off a little steam during the double days.

There were six of us, all sitting in Tom Grainey's Pub off Main Street in the old downtown area, when we all spotted the head coach, our position coach, and two other offensive coaches enter the establishment. The five other guys took off and exited down the stairs to the alternative bar and out through the back way. I stayed seated at my barstool. Later on I would find it to be a costly mistake.

"Why didn't you flee with all the others?" Coach Mass, the defensive back coach, asked me.

"Cause Coach I knew you seen us all and I paid $1.50 for this Budweiser and I intend to finish it."

He smiled and the head coach bought me another Bud, which I sipped. I would later tell my fellow athletes, "The entire coaching staff and I were drinking like old buddies." But the next day at practice, as all the DBs (defensive backs) were stretching, Coach Mass told me to cover each receiver on every wide receiver's route as we practiced one-on-one pass protection.

The sweat was pouring off me. Jimmy Bowden, a strong safety from Compton, California told Coach Mass, "Austen needs to drink some water."

Coach Mass replied, "There's plenty of time for drinking later, right Austen?"

I was so parched I couldn't even respond. I just nodded in agreement.

Finally, Coach gave me the go-ahead to head for the cooler.

Cutting straight across the field I was oblivious to everything else going on. Later I would find out the offensive starters were working on two-minute drills and marching down the field. In my pursuit of quenching my thirst I happen to get blindsided by something. Next thing I knew, I was on the ground. Picking myself off the Boise State green turf, suddenly I was grabbed by Eric Fitzsimmons, the star wide receiver of the Broncos, who also was known as a prima donna who didn't like getting hit. He was the kind of receiver who would get the first down but then step out of bounds to avoid the big hit even though he might have gained another two, or possibly three, yards. It just so happened Fitzsimmons had been running a route and right when he caught the ball I hit him, making him fumble and land on his ass.

All the defensive squad had seen it and was yelling, "Perfect hit, Austen, no pass interference."

Fitzsimmons thought I had purposely cleaned his clock and the fight was on. He grabbed my helmet by the facemask and was having his way with me. I finally figured out what was going on and was able to grab him by the jersey, so down again we both went to the ground. There was no disciplinary action against me based on this occurrence, just the coaches pulling us apart and telling me to watch where I was going.

Later, in the locker room, Coach Mass gave me a high-five and told me, "Excellent hit." He didn't like the offensive players any more than us defensive players did.

So, everything was fine until the fifth game of the year, against the Montana State Bobcats from Bozeman. It was Saturday afternoon and had been snowing since early morning, so there was close to a foot of snow on the sidelines. The field was kept fairly clean but loads of snow were pushed in front of the bleachers. After halftime all of us Broncos came running out from our rest period, where Head Coach

My Bad Tequila

Sorensen had let us have it. He had been yelling, throwing chairs, and verbally abusing some of the starters who had missed an assignment or tackle. Two of the starters had cost us two major penalties of 15 yards each on the same drive, and this had given the Bobcats a three-point lead as they had marched down the field to the 16-yard line and kicked a field goal right before the first half was over. The second half had begun and immediately on the ensuing kickoff, Montana State had run the ball back for an 87-yard touchdown. Some of the crowd in the student section started throwing snowballs and booing the home team. After getting hit with a snowball I scooped up some snow and packed it hard, sending it flying into the stands. The snowball found its mark in the band section, hitting a trumpet, which cut the player's lip and broke his cheekbone. After this the band turned on the team, particularly me and anyone standing next to me. Quite a few players then started throwing snowballs back into the crowd and the campus police had to step in. The game was halted until order was restored, but they had my number (29) and I was hauled into the locker room. We ended up losing the game and I caught hell from my position coach and the head coach for the snowball incident.

But this would not be the end of my football-playing days at BSU; it was the next episode that got me dismissed from the team.

The last home game of the year was against our most hated rivals, the Idaho Vandals from Moscow, Idaho. They had beaten us probably 10 years in a row and this was our year to take them down. Boise State was leading by four points with three minutes left in regulation and we had possession of the ball. It was exciting. I was watching intensely from my great vantage point on the sideline when Head Coach Sorensen came running down the sidelines with headphones on, trying to get the attention of our quarterback. Sorensen was a big man, around 270 pounds and 6'3," and he liked to wear striped shirts all the time. The stripes were not slimming as they were usually blue and orange or the colors of his previous coaching position at Cal Poly State. When it was chilly outside, or during a game, his shirt would be covered with a blue nylon jacket and he always wore those nylon fag-looking pants coaches feel obligated to wear. Anyway, I didn't see Coach S. running down the sideline toward me and before I knew it I was tangled up in the cords from his headset. I tried to untangle myself from the melee but now the cord was completely around my right knee and tightening as the coach continued to run. I was whipped out about five yards onto the field, my knee snapped, and I couldn't get back up quickly enough.

In what looked and sounded like slow motion to me, the r e f e r e e g r a b b e d h i s y e l l o w f l a g, puckered his lips to the silver whistle and I heard the call, "Twwellvve Meeen onn thhe fiellldd, fiivve yaaard pennallttyyy."

What was third down and one yard was now third down and six yards. Needing one more first down to put us in field goal range, the crowd was yelling obscenities at me and the number on my back. I was in agony over my knee and in anguish over the penalty I caused for my Broncos. We only gained four yards on the next play and were then out of field goal range. Our punter was sent in with no great results, touchback, Vandals' ball at their own 20-yard line. There was just a little more than two minutes left and the Vandals drove down the field and scored with 23 seconds left on the board. No miracles on our return kickoff.

Boise State and Austen lose to the University of Idaho by three points.

I was in the trainer's room being examined for my knee, when Sorensen and Mass came up to the table where I'm sitting in pain and looked at my badly swollen knee and Sorensen yells, "How the fuck can one lone stupid ass son-of-a-bitch scout member that is dressed down and not in the game lose the whole fucking game for us?"

Not looking up, I shook my head in shame, while Mass added, "Pack your shit, clean out your locker and turn your jersey, pads and helmet in before you get your knee over to be seen by the team doctor."

The injury was serious but not career ending. My anterior and interior cruciate ligaments were destroyed. I had surgery the following day even though I knew the team doctor did not want to do a successful

My Bad Tequila

surgery. He would have just as soon seen me crippled with a limp for the rest of my life.

Unfortunately, the brace and constant pain in my knee were continuous reminders of the way my number, 29, had been taken away at Bronco Stadium. The worst thing about it was the Idaho Statesman newspaper put me on the front page of the following Sunday sports section and the local television network ran the footage for a week during the sports news segment. There was not a person in the great state of Idaho that did not know of my infamous act.

I was a goat to Boise State fans and a hero to the Idaho Vandals and their followers. I even received two anonymous letters asking me to come play for the Vandal squad. It would be nearly 10 years before BSU would have the opportunity claim victory over the University of Idaho. That was the last time that Boise State played a game on green turf.

When I had returned back to the University from my Christmas break, the turf had been painted a new color blue. Rumors were already swirling that Head Coach Sorensen and the Athletic Director O. Meir (as in Oscar Mayer, pronounced just like the wiener brand) could not get past the image of my trying to scramble off the green Boise turf and needed to do something drastic to remove that agonizing vision. A quick decision by the Board of Regents, accompanied by the go ahead from the high-dollar boosters, and Boise would now have the only blue turf in college football.

That was the end of my college football career in the states.

Which meant my chances of getting laid anytime in the near future were about *nada* (nothing).

But I still had one long shot possibility playing in my head, which might possibly make me an Idaho legend in 25 years. Would this turn of events leading to a blue field possibly jilt the football axis as we know it and allow Boise State University to become the only non BCS Football Program to play for a National Championship?

Author - Rico Austin on Boise State's green field 1985

Boise State Football Team 1985
Author - seated bottom row, second from the right, #29

My Bad Tequila

CHAPTER 4

Leaving Gringo Sanctuary
(Saliendo Santuario Gringo)

I took off my jock strap and shot it with my finger like a rubber band toward my bed in the corner as soon as I entered my shabbily decorated hotel room and closed the door behind me. A nice cool shower was in order before I headed out to Club Med. A couple of divers had told us the "club" existed out of town, towards the north. I turned the faucet labeled "C" for cold but learned very quickly the "C" stood for *caliente*, as in HOT. The "F" stood for Fucking *Frio*, as in cold. I was in the shower for about three minutes when I could have sworn I heard the outside door closing. Towel wrapped around me and dripping wet, I peeked out of the tiny bathroom, but didn't see anyone so I walked to my bed and dug some underwear and a pair of khaki shorts from my duffle bag. The room's only drawer was in the nightstand; one of the scuba boys had already placed dibs on it by putting some clothing inside. I grabbed a wrinkled black Hawaiian-style shirt covered with martini glasses with women in short dresses and high heels in the drinks as stirrers. It was one of my favorites. I put my brace back on, grabbed my money clip, and slipped into my black flip flops. As I walked to the sink with my toothbrush and toothpaste, I thought, "Don't swallow any of the water while brushing." I cleaned my teeth quickly, using very little water, then put on some deodorant and a splash of Brut aftershave.

"Who wants to go to Club Med?" I yelled out of my room at some of the students who were milling about the parking lot.

Tina was the first to respond. "Hell yeah, I'm ready. Let's go," she said as she came running over to give me a high five. Her lavender-flowered sundress skimmed her knees and a small yellow purse hung over her shoulder. Out of the top of her dainty purse was the blue diary, sticking out its head as if it were peering ahead to capture all moments of chosen consideration lest Tina miss them with her pen.

Three other girls said they would join in the adventure as well.

Jennifer and Barbara were juniors who had been best friends since the eighth grade and now studied together at the university. They were sorority sisters too, but I can't remember their particular brand of sisterhood.

When they introduced themselves, I said, "Glad to meet you, Sweet Jenny and Barbie Doll." They hated my little pet names, but they stuck—at least for the Mexico getaway. Jenny had dark short hair in a cute bob and was about 5'7" with great green eyes. Barbie was about an inch shorter than Jenny with medium-long blond hair covered with a baseball hat and a ponytail sticking out the back. Both wore shorts and tank tops. Jenny's shorts were white, and Barbie wore tight jean shorts. They both looked unbelievable, wearing open-toed sandals to show off their freshly painted toes. All the *chicas* (girls) were ecstatic about going on a visit to Club Med.

Mindy had longer auburn hair. She was not stunning like Jenny and Barbie, but more refined looking. I could tell that Mindy and Tina's beauty would continue to develop as they aged and both would be staggering beauties at 50. The other two seemed to be the kind of girls who looked great now but might not be asked to dance at their 30th high school reunion. When reaching that age, they would most likely be heading down the wrinkled road map, starting with their faces then continuing south down to their neck and further below. But for now, I felt lucky to be in their company, all four of them. None of them let on that they knew of my unfortunate football mishap. Of all the girls on the trip it was a tossup for me of who looked hotter, Tina or Barbie. Good fortune was on my side, as they were not sharing a room.

All of the girls, except for Mindy, had tans that looked as if they had been in Mexico for a couple of weeks. I suppose they did the same thing that I and about half of us had done and taken about 10 sessions in a booth at the gym.

Craig came out of his room wearing longer jean shorts, brown sandals and a tank top with the dive symbol plastered on the front. The rear side read, "Divers do it deeper." The dive symbol is a red square with a white stripe from upper hoist to lower fly. This is the "diver down" flag, flown from a boat to tell other ships there is a diver below. The red and white diver-down flag, originally devised about 1957, is intended to help save divers' lives. I thought to myself, "That dive shirt is a beacon to warn girls to stay away from Craig."

Immediately Craig put his arms around both Barbie and Jenny and blurted, "I've got the sorority twins. I'm ready to dance the night away."

I saw Jenny try to slip underneath his arm, but Craig, having been in that awkward circumstance before, had already started to lift his arm away. Barbie just smiled and said, "Me, too."

All three of my bunkmates were coming along as well. Paul Peder (his name fit him well) was the tallest of the three. He was awkward looking and shaped more like a pear than a person, with narrow shoulders and a bit of a paunch. His head seemed to bobble or twitch as he spoke or got ready to speak. He was a cheap bastard even though his family was quite well off. He had a wad of fifties and a couple of Franklins in his pocket that he had pulled out when we had all stopped at the *Cervezateria,* or beer store, to buy cases of bottled Mexican beer. All four of us had decided to share the cost of four cases of Corona and four cases of Pacifico. But once we were at the counter Paul changed his mind, saying he probably would only drink 24 beers instead of 48 so he wanted to discount his contribution.

I didn't say anything as I didn't know the guys that well, but the other two spoke up. "Paul, for heaven's sake, don't start this again," one said. "You do this every time we agree to split the cost."

His other friend said what I was already thinking. "You cheapass, just reach into your pocket and pay your share, besides you'll most likely drink more than any of us." Then he added, "Right Rhet?"

I was caught off guard but managed to say, "Yeah, let's just stick with the original plan."

Paul slapped his share of the money onto the counter, but I noticed he took extra time counting his change and used a calculator to make sure things were square.

"Good luck in the real world," I wanted to say to Paul and his two sidekicks, all seniors and planning to graduate in May with Business Administration degrees.

The other two scuba pals didn't seem too bad. I could bear living and sharing close quarters for five days with them. The shortest of the three was Marcus Williams, who was about 5'7" with dark hair he wore almost in a crew cut. He looked the most athletic of the three, which is not to say a lot about their physique. He also talked the most, even though Paul seemed to be their leader. The other scuba pal was Theodore. I couldn't believe he still went by his given name; I had tried to call him Teddy twice, but he corrected me both times, and said, "My name is Theodore," in a somewhat sophisticated manner.

So, Theodore it was; anyhow for now.

Two other guys who were friends before the trip came, too. They stayed pretty much to themselves. They were hippie types with longer hair who had been wearing long Mexican shirts since leaving

My Bad Tequila

Boise. Both had beads and necklaces around anything they could hang them off of: their neck, wrists, ankles, toes and fingers. Matz and Ritchie is what they called each other. This worked for me.

In total we had the four girls going, my three roommates, Craig, the two hippie dudes and me, which made eleven of us heading out. I walked to the first room, the one that served as an office, and asked Luis to call us a couple of taxis.

"San Carlos no have taxi, Señor Rhet," he said.

"So, Luis, how do we get to Club Med?"

"You need to catch ride or take the bus Señor Rhet."

He told me where we could catch the local bus and the cost, two pesos per rider. Walking back to the group I told them of our ride dilemma.

Tina spoke up, "No *problema porque yo hablo Español* (No problem because I speak Spanish). Besides it'll be fun."

We all agreed to do it and started walking slowly from the partially paved parking lot to the dusty gravel street and down the winding hill towards town. Sunset was nearly over and the sky had started to darken as we made our way to the main street where we would catch the bus. Mostly everyone was laughing and talking during the half-mile hike. We found the bus stop where there were no other people waiting to catch the bus. Across the street and down about fifty yards was the bus stop heading the other direction towards Guaymas, and there five Mexican locals were waiting.

Guaymas is approximately eight miles from San Carlos and is much larger than the Seaside resort town. Guaymas has a large fishing port with dozens and dozens of shrimping boats in and about the harbor. Most of the Mexicans that work in San Carlos live in Guaymas because land is much less expensive and it is where their families were born and raised. Most of the residents in San Carlos are retired Americans and Canadians and a very few select rich Mexicans.

We had been waiting about five minutes when I spotted a badly dented red Chevy pickup truck with a heavily cracked windshield on the passenger's side; it was heading our way with three young Mexican guys in it. Already tired of waiting for the bus I jumped out into the street and started waving the same way I had seen it done by carless Mexicans during our trek down from the States. The Chevy pulled up to the stop, and the driver and two passengers looked a bit surprised at all the college-aged *gringo* kids standing at the bus stop.

"*Americanos?*" asked the driver.

"*Si,*" Tina answered without hesitation. "*Nosotros esperamos ir a Club Med, por favor*" (We're waiting to go to Club Med, please).

The driver, who spoke a little Spanglish, nodded, "*Amigos*, get in *mi carro*" (my car).

Tina and I jumped in the bed of the truck but the others were frozen in place. Craig blurted, "I don't think it's a good idea; let's just wait for the bus."

"We're going to Club Med, who wants to go now?" I asked. "Or you can wait for who knows how much longer for the bus."

Barbie and Jenny crawled in, and so did the hippie twosome and Theodore. But not before Paul told him, "I agree with Craig, please wait for the bus."

Tina leaned over into the cab on the passenger side, "*Nosotros listo. Vamos.*" (We're ready. Let's go). And off we went, leaving Craig, two of the scuba babies, and Mindy behind.

My Bad Tequila

CHAPTER 5

Club Med
(Club de Med)

Club Med, on the outskirts of San Carlos in Sonora, Mexico, was the true beginning of "MY BAD TEQUILA," a phrase I coined a few months after returning back to Idaho from Spring Break. Each of us has our own "My Bad Tequila,"—something horrible and/or bizarre that has happened to you. It may be world renowned, or it may be a hidden, dark secret that only one, two, or a handful of people know of the damning occurrence.

Until Mexico "MY BAD TEQUILA" would have been something minor, as in getting slightly grazed in the shoulder by a crazy native Shoshone Indian woman firing a 45-caliber Colt Revolver at an after-hours party in the lumberjack country of the Sawtooths in Stanley, Idaho near the Sun Valley and Ketchum area. It could have been getting a DUI in Portland, Oregon after rear-ending an off-duty police officer fresh off his shift and heading home for the evening. Or it could have been losing an ear in a bar fight over a pool game on the island of Kauai, Hawaii. All of which have the making of a great story, but none of which compare to my Mexico Getaway.

"MY BAD TEQUILA." Had it been a little less bad, might not have haunted me for all these years.

If I had not gone on that trip, if I had just opted to wait a few minutes more for the local bus and put my two *pesos* into the tin box. If I had not flagged down the pickup truck. If…

There are so many ifs that if just one thing had been done differently the outcome of several of our lives, including my own, would have been different. I now believe in physics and in the complete power of physics. Even though I refused to take it in my undergraduate studies I know more about physics than I wish to know. Newton's Third Law of Motion states, "for every action, there is an equal and opposite reaction."

"MY BAD TEQUILA" was in infancy when I made the decision to leave Boise and handed over to Craig my first installment of $75.00 for the trip. My choosing to do so, and the choices I continued to make while on "vacation" have impacted several people, some of them strangers, some of them not so strange. And, of course, "MY BAD TEQUILA" affected me and would later affect my family and friends.

The narrow road to the Club Mediterranean sets off a friendly yet slightly eerie welcome. The resort, six miles from San Carlos, is surrounded by the natural beauty of over two-and-a-half miles of sandy beach. It boasts all the necessary elements for a secluded relaxation or activity-filled experience to be recalled for years to come. The choice is yours.

Where the desert and the mountains meet the sea…That is the way it is advertised today as Paradiso Resort. Great line.

Club Med in San Carlos is nestled between the mountains of the Sonoran Desert and the deep blue waters of the Sea of Cortez. The resort boasts a unique landscape of cacti and red desert rock mountains towering over an azure lagoon.

I recall vividly the ride up the winding road, then back down again to where the panga boats parked in the muddy, stagnant lagoon waters. All of us were looking at each other, wondering with great anticipation of what adventures lay ahead.

I was a bit nervous by the rapid acceleration of the pickup after we had climbed into the bed. It still is a mystery to me, why life in Mexico always so slow but as soon as you climb into or on a motorized vehicle, suddenly life speeds up and there is no such thing as a slow lane? From that first experience as a traveler with a Mexican operator at the wheel, it has always been the same, as fast as possible. Whether it was with a taxi driver, a Mexican *amigo* or lifting a ride with a local stranger; no time to waste. As soon as the engine starts, Mexican time is no longer the same.

We passed the lagoon on the right along with an open-air restaurant; to this day I have not passed through its threshold. There cannot be any humanly way possible that an enjoyable meal or drink could be consumed with the Minnesota-sized mosquitoes swarming about the waist deep water that the eatery is sided with.

Our driver friend barely slowed for the curve as we entered a residential area with homes on both sides of the street. If anyone, human or house pet, had happened to cross in front of our careening vehicle I most likely would not be writing and sharing this story. At the very least we would have been in an infirmary listening to Paul and Craig saying, "I told you not to get in that pickup truck."

We safely made it through the corridor and onto the other side of the great Tetakawi Mountain, where we saw crystal blue water with the nearly full moon shining on it like a postcard. We were now getting close to our destination as all life was disappearing and we could see a bunch of lights ahead of us—Club Med. Then just like that all the lights were gone again as giant palms and acres and acres of cacti blocked the twinkling.

Right before we entered the long desolate cobblestone driveway there was an old wooden sign that warned, "Catch 22 dees way."

"Oh my gosh, this is the place my Grandpa told me about," Barbie blurted.

Before I could ask what she meant, Barbie launched into a dissertation about a great movie that originated from a great novel. Most great books or narrations later evolve into eternal films, and those of us who've never read them believe the movie started it all.

Barbie explained in detail that the sign pointing towards the landing strip was made for the movie. Her explanation went something like this: "Catch-22 is a satirical, historical novel by the American author Joseph Heller, first published in 1961. The novel, set during the later stages of World War II, is frequently cited as one of the great literary works of the twentieth century. It has a distinctive non-chronological, style where events are described from different characters' points of view and out of sequence so that the timeline develops along with the plot."

She continued to tell us that "Part of the movie was filmed in San Carlos and was released in the United States on June 24, 1970 and directed by Mike Nichols. Screenplay was written by Buck Henry who also starred in the movie as the Lieutenant Colonel Korn. The film was later released in the United Kingdom on September 17, 1970 and then in dozens of more countries around the globe."

Without missing a beat Barbie concluded with "Initially it was a bit of a bomb, earning less acclaim and *dinero* than MASH, another war-themed black comedy also released in 1970. In subsequent years, though, opinions of Catch-22 have been revised and it is now seen as one of the great satirical anti-war films."

When Barbie finished her oration, I saw her in a whole new light. "Wow," I thought. "This chick has it all, brains and a knockout body." Theodore beat me to the question of how she was so informed about Catch-22. She answered, nonchalantly, that her grandfather had been an actor in it.

Barbie Doll sure knew how to draw a crowd into a story and save the best for last. I knew this instantly by the way she had reeled us all in.

My Bad Tequila

In unison we all echoed each other, "Who was he? Would we know him?"

"You might," she hinted. I could tell she was feeling pretty full of herself now, but hell, so would I if my grandfather had been a movie star.

"Have any of you heard of Norman Fell?" she finally asked.

"Norman Fell," I thought, "How could this doll be related to Norman Fell?" Before anyone else could answer, I stated matter-of-factly, "Wasn't he in the sitcom 'Three's Company' with John Ritter and Suzanne Somers?"

"That's right," she said, with what looked like admiration for my quick response.

I liked where this was headed. "He played Mr. Roper, the apartment complex manager," I added.

Not everyone in the back of the truck looked impressed with my quick recall of the sitcom. It was a good thing she hadn't said Bob Denver as I never would have stopped talking about my favorite actor growing up: the famous castaway, Gilligan.

I added three more items to my to-do-list: Have sex—or at least try to make out with—the granddaughter of a movie star on the runway where filming had taken place, then read the book and see the movie.

The conversation had ended as we turned left onto a rough cobblestone roadway surrounded by cacti. It looked a little spooky as we approached the guard gate. The pathway leading to the entrance was lined entirely with cacti, mostly saguaro, some senita, a few cardon and slightly more organ pipe cactus. It immediately reminded me of the film "The Shining" with Jack Nicholson as the maniac caretaker. Only this was cacti and not pine trees as was the case in the movie featuring "The Timberline Lodge" on Mt. Hood in Oregon.

To this day my friends and I refer to the "old Club Med" as "The Shining."

Our *amigo*, the same driver who could have easily tossed us all to the concrete or asphalt road, sped to the entry way and stopped on a *peso*.

"*Bienvenidos a* (Welcome to) Club Med," the old man at the guard shack proudly proclaimed as we halted in front of his home away from home for 14 hours each day, six days a week.

"*Nosotros aqui para la fiesta! Estas personas de Estados Unidos en mi carro!*" There is no translation needed as everyone knows that (We are here for the party! These people are from the United States in my car!)

We all waved and said, "*Muchas Gracias,*" as the old gray-haired *Mexicano* motioned us in at the same time he lifted the metal gate that separated us from an eternity of memories. In we went.

Passing hundreds of empty parking spots, past the soccer fields, baseball playing fields, and any other field that you could come up with, we neared the front entrance and could see several tour buses.

Tina was the first to jump ship as she cleared the sideboards and everything else that Chevy had conjectured up to keep a wild woman inside its bed.

Shouting, "*Arriba Mexico,*" as she hit the cobblestone driveway she enlightened all of us and brought us back to the *fiesta* mood. She lost her left flat but as quickly as I saw it, I had forgotten it. Not my problem.

Our new taxi friends were eager to celebrate. I was nearly sober now, thanks to the walk and our crazy ride.

Barbie leapt from the back of the truck as if she were a trapeze artist. I was next to jump and felt a twang of pain as I landed, still holding onto the side rail.

Theodore was closest to the tailgate and exiting when the tailgate crumpled under him. He hit the stones hard, bouncing nearly an inch-and-a-half before settling. I saw his wrist bone, clear and white, pop the freckled skin between his arm and hand with a crimson wave of blood washing after.

At the same instant Matz, who had been leaning against the tailgate, came tumbling out, most of his weight landing on Teddy's arm and injured wrist.

My Bad Tequila

Everything went into slow motion as Matz bounced off Theodore and rolled onto the jagged cobblestones, which previously had seemed so flat and well placed. Teddy screamed once more as his dislocated and badly broken wrist bone hit the hard, dirty surface. I cringed, as did everyone else. We had all witnessed the same thing and were now sick to our stomachs.

Reaction came first from Tina who slipped into the shoe that she had lost, pulled a handkerchief from her small purse, and gently slipped it onto Teddy's wrist. As soon as the hanky found its spot it was scarlet red and smelled of blood. "Thank God we are not in the ocean," was the only thought I could muster.

I ran into the *oficina* (office) and asked for a doctor. Luckily, the word doctor in Spanish is pronounced almost the same as English, just with a little more emphasis on the second "O".

The manager on duty spoke a little English and told me they did have a doctor on the premises. I pointed to the parking lot and said, "Accident, my *amigo* is hurt." I was getting ready to head back to the parking place when I saw the group huddled around Theodore and walking him to the building I was about to exit.

Theodore's entourage got him into the office and onto a couch set in front of the large glass window. Ice arrived via a beautiful young *senorita* with jet black hair, dark brown eyes, and perfect olive skin. I felt guilty checking out the "nurse" while poor Teddy agonized in unrelenting pain, but I couldn't help myself. She was *perfecto*.

The doctor showed within five minutes, excellent time for Mexico. He spoke brilliant English with a Mexican accent. I later heard he also spoke French and German perfectly.

He looked at Theodore's wrist and poured on a healthy dose of hydrogen peroxide to clean the wound; this was contrary to what the old Western movies filmed in Mexico showed. The victim was always doused with tequila to sterilize the wound and then the unfortunate person was given at least two double shots of tequila to ease the pain. The "*ambulancia*" showed up at about the same time as did the other four of our group that had elected to wait on the bus.

Paul and Marcus were badly shaken from the incident and both gave me an evil glance that said they put the blame squarely on my broad shoulders.

Teddy was given a shot for the pain, then strapped down and taken to the hospital in Hermosillo 90 miles away. The driver had a legitimate reason to speed. Another *hombre* sat in the passenger seat who must have been the father of the nine-year-old next to him. Or perhaps the boy was a very young apprentice. This was another example of why I love Mexico, there is almost always something happening out of the ordinary, such as a kid riding around all night in an ambulance.

Marcus and Paul took the next bus back into San Carlos and said they would hitch a ride to Hermosillo with the chaperone dad who had the suburban.

"Damn," I thought, "Three vacations ruined." But, on the positive side, I suddenly had a room to myself.

All of us were left standing in the breezeway next to the main office. On one side of the wall was a huge world map pinpointing all the Club Meds around the globe. On the other side of the breezeway wall was a huge activities board that showed the different times for each activity. There was a time designated for each, including but not limited to softball, badminton, football (soccer), water polo, basketball, swimming lessons, dancing, water aerobics, fishing in the pond, fishing off the beach, horseback riding, hiking to Nacapuli Canyon, snorkeling, even scuba diving classes and instruction. Next to the large activities board was another large glass picture window showcasing all the equipment available to check out. If you wanted to play catcher on the softball field, there was a catcher's mask, vest, and shin guards along with the mitt. This was an incredible place, a jock's dream world. I did not know such places existed.

There was supposed to be a $20.00 cover charge which included some snacks, and "*bedidas nacionales*," (national drinks)— premixed *piña coladas* and margaritas on the rocks made with some of the worst and ripest agave in the country of Mexico mixed to make the

My Bad Tequila

cheapest tequila in the world. I guess since we had the great *accidente* the attendants in the office felt bad and waved all of us through except the three Mexican dudes who had transported us here. Tina spoke to the beautiful senorita and the little skinny Mexican man in Spanish and told of our a*migos*' plight. The office staff hesitated, but when we all in unison cried out, "let our *amigos* in," they relented and no longer created a barrier for our dark-haired brown friends.

Craig, once again in charge, led the way to paradise. We passed two swimming pools, both skillfully tiled. The first seemed to be a lap pool with a blue and green tiled giant tortoise on the bottom. It was much deeper than the next pool which had 1.1 meter etched onto its sides. A group was playing pool volleyball as we walked past on the way to the large open-aired bar. There were tanned bodies everywhere, some in bathing suits and some in shorts and T-shirts or tank tops.

"Oh my gosh," I gushed, as I saw what must have been two European chicks without tops, and just a couple of strings to cover their "no no spots." You know the place I'm speaking of, the place where you're told as a toddler to not touch your "no no spot."

Back when I was growing up, child molesters were a lot fewer or maybe we just never heard about them since there was not an Internet or the good law that requires "Chester the Molester" to notify the neighbors when he moves into the area. In today's times kids are told by their parents that teachers, friends, relatives, and strangers alike should never touch their "no no spots." And if for shame this does occur, "please tell us right away." Great strategy to have.

Anyway, I could not believe my eyes, nor could the other students, both guys and girls. This was something we had never witnessed up in the North Country. I tried hard not to stare as I did not want Barbie and Tina especially to think this was my "first rodeo."

Most of us lingered in the pool area a bit longer before making it into the large bar section with gorgeous mesquite wooden floors. I headed straight for the *palapa* bar on the other side of the play pool for three reasons. There were not as many young adults hanging near this bar waiting for drinks. Secondly, I was able to let my eyes soak up the eye candy a bit longer, particularly the *chicas* (girls) without tops. Lastly, I needed to ditch Tina because I wanted Barbie *esta noche* (tonight).

"What are you looking at?" my ears heard a female voice questioning.

Surprised and somewhat embarrassed I turned to see that Barbie had also made her way to the *palapa* bar and was now standing next to me with her backside leaning against the bar. My slight blush faded and I responded, "*chi chis*" (tits). This Spanish word I had known since I was an eighth grader or so.

Barbie smiled and gave me a huge long-lasting wink notifying me via flirtation that everything was going to be great. I ordered us both margaritas. As I handed over hers she put her soft tan hand on mine and held it for half a second before taking the mixed concoction from my stiffened fingers.

I looked hard into Barbie's adventure-seeking blue eyes while purposely licking my tongue over my lips that had started to already dry just a day into Mexico. She knew I wanted her and was not intimidated by her beauty.

There was music playing and it seemed to be coming from the inside the building. With a great deal of confidence, I leaned over near Barbie's ear and quietly said, "Let's finish this margarita and go dance."

I was lucky growing up that my brothers and I were forbidden to dance by our mother and her religious standards. Since dancing was taboo, whenever we boys were alone we would turn on the radio, a record, or an 8-track and dance our asses off. We secretly watched American Bandstand and knew every dance, move, and groove that had been done in the free world. Since it was just us and no other onlookers, we were never embarrassed, and we danced with gusto. Over the years we all became good, confident dancers.

My first dance was my junior prom, which was also my senior prom since I graduated high school as a junior at the age of sixteen. I sped my education up so I might become the assistant manager and get more hours at the local grocery store. This would allow me to help my

My Bad Tequila

family with the monthly trailer rent and bills.

At the prom I surprised everyone, including my date, with my dancing ability. My classmates knew I was forbidden to dance, and I'm sure in my light green checkered suit they expected me to sip punch all night and sit on the edge of the auditorium stage, in awe of their dancing. That green checkered suit, a major JCPenney purchase, was to be first worn at my high school graduation. After that fun and memorable evening of dancing with Jana, a girl that I had known since moving to Marsing in the seventh grade, my new suit was soiled with the endless drops of perspiration that had separated themselves from my glands that night. The next time I wore it was after I had picked up my first garment from a dry-cleaning store in nearby Homedale. That was the first and last time I danced in that suit or in that town.

Barbie and I gulped down our tequila-laden drinks. I grabbed her hand and we bolted toward the large building. On our way in we saw Craig and Mindy sitting at the long wooden bar, crowded into a spot made for only one person. Barbie said exactly what I was thinking. "Poor Mindy."

We neared the far end of the bar at the back of the building towards the sea where the grand room had been sectioned off by lounge chairs, couches, and a couple of TVs. Beyond this there were pool tables and foosball tables, most of them in full use by the guests. At this point we could see and hear where the music was originating.

We entered through an over-sized French door opening that was missing the extra wide doors. It looked to me as if the latches had been permanently removed. A Mexican rock band was playing an Eagles tune. The music sounded great, and the lead singer's strong accent gave a strange flavor to the song. The room was grandiose with the constant flow of mesquite flooring from the bar and main restaurant. All other flooring was of an off-white marble tile with streaks of dark color resembling lightning streaks in a thunderstorm. A large wooden stage that ran almost the entire length in the back of the auditorium hosted the five-piece band and singer with just one lone giant microphone clasped in both hands as he bellowed out the

"Welkeem toodeee Otel Caleefornia."

I glanced around the room for an empty table on the outskirts of the ballroom-sized dance floor, but saw none, so I led Barbie out to the dance floor; we danced to the rhythm of the sound. The song ended and I saw Matz and Jenny walking off the floor towards a table where some of our other comrades were already sitting. Ritchie was there, Tina, and two of the Mexicans who had driven us to this mecca. Tina saw us and motioned for us to join them. "Damn, there goes my plan," I grimaced secretly inside while smiling on the outside.

We hadn't formally introduced ourselves to our new-found *amigos*, so I extended my hand to the one who had been sitting in the middle of the truck, since he was nearest to me. I practiced my broken Spanglish. "*Me llamo* (I am called) Rhet, nice to meet you, and this pretty *senorita* (young girl) is Barbie." I don't even think that counts as Spanglish, the first part of the sentence in Spanish and the majority in English.

He replied, "*Me llamo Juan, mucho gusto*" (glad to meet you). I said in return, "*Mucho gusto.*"

Turning toward the other *muchacho* (young man), who had been riding shotgun, I repeated my phrase once again. His name was Guillermo and said that his special name (nickname) was Mamo and that we might all call him that as it was easier for gringos to say. His English was close to being good and he seemed happy to be able to speak. Juan seemed as if he understood English well but was not comfortable speaking, so he nodded continuously to conversations, mimicking a bobble-head doll. Tina was speaking to both of them in their native tongue as she wanted to practice her language skills.

The band was once again making music, singing, in English, an old Beatles tune, "I Want to Hold Your Hand." I saw Tina glance my way just for a second but before I could react Barbie was pulling me towards the stage for a second dance.

Barbie and I were beginning to dirty dance even though this style of dancing didn't match the music. The floor was packed with a twenty to early-thirties crowd. Someone bumped into my behind hard enough I turned to see. Tina was there dancing with Juan and smiling infectiously. I tried to ignore her and concentrate on Barbie. But, like a bull elk that has to have more than one cow, I wanted both of them. I was about to leave the safety of shore and was swimming out to treacherous waters.

I moved strategically around the dance floor so as to watch Barbie and Tina move simultaneously. Fortunately for me, Barbie was into the song and closed her eyes for a few seconds at a time. The song ended and another began. We stayed on the dance floor but my eyes followed Tina's nice rump back to her table.

Thirsty again, Barbie and I headed back out to the *palapa* bar for a refill on our unlimited refreshments. More hard bodies were at the *palapa* bar now and the alcohol was doing its job of taking the shyness away, as was obvious by several couples now touching and kissing each other. To my pleasure there were five topless girls and two of them were sitting on the shoulders of their "camels" as camel fights (also known as chicken fights depending upon what part of the United States you belong to) had now begun in the pool where volleyball had once been the game of choice.

Barbie made it easy for me to look as she too was fascinated by this over-exposure of skin and body.

Pressing my body next to hers I proposed, "I'll let you ride on my shoulders if you take off your top."

Her response took me by surprise. "If I take off my top, I want to be riding on more than just your shoulders."

I could think of no quick reply, so I let go with a fake chuckle that probably resembled nervousness. Needing to reevaluate my game I excused myself to use the *baño* (bathroom) and scurried off like an inexperienced, frightened schoolboy. Safely in the restroom I went to the sink and splashed massive amounts of cool water on my face and neck while smiling at my reflection. I was quite proud of myself. I dried my face and marched back to the bar, chest fully puffed and full.

When I returned, two young men that had bodies and muscles of body builders had turned their attentions and affections upon my lovely Barbie Doll. Acting as if I hadn't noticed, I ordered a Corona for us both while pulling my money clip from my pocket, giving the bartender a two-dollar tip for added emphasis. This seemed to work as both of them were now looking at me instead of Barbie and half-heartedly introduced themselves before slithering off for new prey.

We found a couple of empty stools next to the bar and made them our own. We made a little chit-chat, saying what a great place this was, etcetera, etcetera. I motioned to the bartender with my finger that we needed another round.

Sliding off my stool I leaned close to Barbie and gave her a peck on the cheek, and then another. She must have liked it because before I knew it our lips were pressing hard against the other's mouth and our tongues were searching for something more in new and unfamiliar territory. I took a breath just long enough to whisper, "Let's go to the beach." I had already forgotten about my goal of finding the old airstrip of Catch-22 with Barbie. All I could think of was holding the precious flesh that made up this heavenly angel named Barbara.

We separated our tongues and faces. Now joined by our hands, my right and her left, as we made our way back to the main building and down the large corridor to the monstrous opening in the rear, where all that met the eye was shimmering sea and light-colored sand on the beach. The moon was nearly full. In two more nights it would be in all its glory.

Swinging our arms, while holding onto each other's entwined fingers, we walked on the beach towards the edge of the sand. We both kicked off our footwear as we neared where the sea encountered the visible Earth. I grabbed my shoes and then Barbie's and ran them back towards the building to keep them dry. A few seconds later I was back with the girl, arms around her and kissing her face madly but softly.

A hundred yards or so down the shore was a bonfire. We could see the shadows and outlines of what looked to be about 50 people. Barbie and I headed in the opposite direction after separating our bodies again. Barbie seemed to be stumbling quite a bit and giggling over almost anything I would say or do. After walking for three or four

My Bad Tequila

minutes I let myself plop some thirty yards from the sea onto millions of tiny particles of sand, which made for a very cushioned landing. Barbie followed suit and again our mouths found each other.

Lying down, my back pressed into the sand, Barbie climbed onto me, straddling me while sitting on my lower stomach. She fumbled with my shirt, got it unbuttoned completely, and started rubbing my chest, occasionally giving it a quick, wet kiss.

I had pulled her top off and was just beginning to unhook her bra strap when she started to say something I couldn't quite make out, that sounded like, "I'm gonna, I'm goin."

Without any warning other than the four words I heard, Barbie orally ejected all beverages consumed that afternoon and evening directly onto me. I took the full force of her stomach's rejection in the face, all over my chest, neck, shoulders, arms and stomach.

Pushing Barbie off me and into the sand, I shrieked, "What the hell are you doing?"

I rolled over and started to jump to my feet when I noticed that Barbie wasn't moving. No longer angry or disgusted by the smell or the occurrence, I shook Barbie to make sure she was alive. Thank goodness, she half-heartedly grunted, and I knew she was breathing. She had passed out as soon as her body had rolled over into the dry, cool sand and was in a comatose state.

I made sure that Barbie was on her side, so as not to choke on her own vomit should her insides again decide to spew. Using her top, I made a makeshift pillow for her head to help keep sand out of her hair. I grabbed my now-not-so-favorite shirt, found a dry, clean area and wiped Barbie's mouth and chin. She had completely missed getting any of the vile substance on herself; it all had come to rest on me and my clothing.

Still holding my shirt, I walked straight for the Sea of Cortez and took off my khaki shorts, which had managed to dodge Barbie's vomit. I did not want to expose my wallet and money to water. Stripped down to my underwear and knee brace, I entered the cool, refreshing, salty water. Oh, it felt great as I rinsed and rinsed again my shirt, my body, my face, and my hair.

I had been in the water probably about five minutes, just enjoying the salty smell and seeing the moon high in the heavens, when a sharp pain hit my upper leg, then another. "Shit," I thought aloud. "What was that?" My mind was racing, thinking of all the horrible, nasty creatures in the sea that would want a part of me or maybe all of me. I made my way out as quickly as possible, trying not to panic, as visions of sharks, stingrays, moray eels, and giant octopuses made their way through my tunneled one-track mind. Just as I was about to exit the sea I saw the "blue bastard" that had stung me.

"Thank goodness," I whispered, and again felt the sharp pangs returning. I was trying to see what damage the lone jellyfish had done to my leg when all thoughts and actions were interrupted by a scream and a voice yelling, "Get off me, get off me, you, you..."

Another scream.

I turned to where the scream had come from and saw a figure running away towards the building. Now the person in distress was pleading for someone to help.

My heart sank as I recognized the voice.

No longer feeling the sting, I ran as quickly as I could in the sand and with the steel contraption clinging to my leg and knee. Barbie was sobbing, her shorts down close to her knees, but her panties still on.

She was topless, the bra no longer covering her up. I threw my wet shirt around her, which was not the wisest thing to do as she began shaking violently and seemed to be entering into hysteria. I spotted her top, picked it up, put it on her, and tossed mine to the sand.

Not knowing what to do, I put my arms around Barbie and tried to quiet her. No one else had heard her screams and I don't know how long she had been pleading for rescue as I had been enjoying myself in the sea. She started to quiet and her shivering had calmed immensely.

Barbie began to sob quietly. "Where were you?" she asked in between shallow gasps. "Why did you leave me alone?" Her questions sounded as if coming from a child, not this fully shaped woman who just minutes earlier had seemed so self-assured, ready to take on anything or anybody.

I didn't know where to start or what to share. "I'm sorry, I'm so sorry, Barbie." I managed to choke out the words. "You threw up on me and I went to the ocean to get cleaned up."

Barbie began frantically hitting me in the chest. "You left me! You left me alone on the beach! Alone by myself!" She was now crying vehemently and again near hysterics.

I grabbed her wrists to stop the pounding and then pulled her close while repeating my apologies and sympathy. "I'm sorry, so sorry. I didn't think that…"

She cut me off in midsentence. "That's right, you didn't think. You're an asshole, just thinking of yourself. Oh, poor you, you got puked on, poor you."

I felt better as I continued to hold her. At least she was now angry, no longer sobbing in complete distress. Again, I apologized.

Quite calm now, Barbie apologized for her last outburst and added, "I was just scared and didn't know what was happening."

I started asking questions.

"Did you see who it was?"

"Were you," I hesitated midsentence, "raped?"

Surprisingly, Barbie answered quickly and with lack of strong emotion, "No, I didn't see who it was. I woke up; some guy was laying part way on me or next to me pulling down my shorts and my top was off."

She then slowly pulled the question out. "Did, did you take my top and bra off?"

I answered slowly. "I did take your top off you when we were making out, after you had unbuttoned and started trying to take my shirt off." I then added, "I did not take off your bra, don't you remember what happened?"

"No, not really," Barbie answered shyly.

"Well, thank goodness you have a great set of lungs, no pun

intended." We both laughed.

"I had better go grab my shorts, my wallet and money are with them. I'll be right back, Okay?" I trotted through the sand to locate my belongings.

"Okay, but hurry," she called softly.

The pain of the sting was getting worse. I was starting to feel the pain spread into my groin and my abdomen. I felt sick, really sick; however, I decided not to say anything to Barbie.

I returned with shorts on and shook my sandy shirt before donning it. We found our shoes and walked back towards the building. I asked Barbie if she was physically okay and if she needed or wanted to see the in-house physician who had cared for Teddy earlier.

She declined and said she wanted to go warm herself beside the fire on the beach. This sounded like a great idea, so we walked on the beach once more; however, she would not take my hand as we made our way towards the gigantic flame and the half-naked bodies.

After reaching the safe flames which cast light upon the surrounding beach and glistening sea, we spotted Jenny. Barbie ran to her. I joined them and turned to Barbie, looking her in the eyes as I told her, "Listen, I'll be right back. I need to use the little boys' room and I'll get you a Sprite."

Barbie, feeling safe and a lot warmer now, gave me a dirty look as she told me she would be all right and added, "Take your time."

I assured her I would be back in an instant and headed for the bar, where I asked for a Corona, a tequila shot, and a Sprite. The bartender gave me the first two, along with a Squirt. I then questioned him concerning my jellyfish sting. He reached underneath the bar as if for a fresh bottle of tequila or rum but produced a spray bottle, like the kind you would use when ironing. Armando—I could see the name tag clipped to his white uniform—handed me the bottle and instructed me to spray it on my wounds.

"What is it?" I asked while spraying it on my upper leg, where two giant welts were spreading.

"Veeneeger, Senor, is very good for thee sting."

My Bad Tequila

"*Gracias*," I replied, handing the bottle back along with a five spot for his knowledge of treating jellyfish bites and his excellent bedside manner.

When I returned to the bonfire, Barbie was still clinging to Jenny's side. I handed Barbie her Squirt. Mexico has an abundance of Squirt as the Mexicans mix it with tequila over ice to make an instant margarita.

This seemed like a great time to make my exit as I was still feeling quite uneasy from the vibes given off by Barbie and Jenny. I also felt queasy from the sting, my midsection especially. I'd had enough excitement for one evening. I told Barbie and Jenny I was heading back to the room as I didn't feel all that well.

"Oh, had too much to drink, did we?" Jenny teased.

"Yeah, somethin' like that." I managed a half grin. "Adios *amigas* and please be safe." I headed back inside for another spray of Armando's vinegar and another shot of tequila, followed by a Mexican beer chaser with lime.

On the way back to the bar, my eye caught Tina coming out the *baño* door that read "*Senoritas*." She saw me and I motioned her towards the bar. She met me there and asked where my new girlfriend Barbie was. I ignored her question and asked her what she cared to drink.

"I'll have a Diet Coke," she said, then added, "por favor" (please) to Armando.

"Still not drinking very much, even though we're on vacation?" I asked.

"No, alcohol never really agreed with me, and besides I don't need it for a good time."

"You're right, you don't need it, but, man, I do." I chuckled slightly.

"Soooo, were you surprised to see me on the bus?" Tina asked in a sexy tone, running her fingers through her hair on the right side.

"Damn right I was, but just as surprised that you really haven't spoken to me," I retorted back in a half-playful, half-serious tone.

"Armando, *otra* (another) Corona, *por favor* and another shot of your vinegar."

Tina looked at me, puzzled yet amused, and asked, "When did you start drinking vinegar?"

I grabbed the spray bottle before the beer bottle, which in my case was very odd behavior. I sprayed my welts, which were starting to resemble a reddish rash, and exhaled. The pain subsided gradually, and my bowels felt as if they might function properly in the near future.

She then said, "I thought it was the other way around, you weren't being sociable to me. You do know, don't you, that when you mentioned to me that you were going on this Spring Break trip I got to thinking I might go as well."

"Why didn't you tell me you were thinking about it?" I questioned.

"A couple of reasons. One, I was afraid you might not want me to go, and two, I thought it might be a nice surprise." She added hesitantly, "There is one more reason, which I'll tell you a little later, towards the end of the trip."

"Well, I'm glad you're here, you little secret agent. *Salud* (Cheers)." I raised my bottle to touch Tina's plastic cup with ice and Diet Coke.

I told Tina I was on my way out to catch a taxi as the jellyfish had got the best of our meeting in the sea. The only person I had known before taking this trip asked if she could share the ride and fare.

We were off to our hotel in San Carlos.

We sat in silence for most of the taxi ride in a small white Ford. As the driver approached the hotel, we split the cab fare. I walked Tina to her room, told her I was glad she was in Mexico with me, and gave her a long goodnight kiss, then walked fairly straight to my room.

Upon entering, I took off my damp underwear and shirt, placed my brace beside the bed, put on clean, dry underwear, and climbed underneath the sheets and the Mexican blanket. I lay there wondering about my roommates, how they were doing and where they were as I drifted off into a restless sleep filled with nightmares.

Person: What's it like to party with you?
Rico: Well, it's a bit like a merry-go-round
Person: Oh that sounds like fun!
Rico: I'm not finished...

CHAPTER 6

The Snorkeling and Dive Trip
(Viaje de Tubo de Respiracion y Buseo)

The next morning, I awoke to pounding on the door of my room. "Fuck me," I said aloud, as I knew I had overslept.

Our day had been planned out. Some of us were going snorkeling and the more skilled were going diving. I leapt from my bed, only to feel a jolt of pain on my right side. Not fully awake and startled, I had not secured the contraption that helped hold my knee in place.

"Aaugh," I shrieked, and another loud rap at the door sounded. "Just a minute," I yelled as I put on my brace and a pair of shorts.

I opened the door to find a smiling Tina, standing there in a pair of bright yellow, cotton shorts that read "Corona" and a black bikini top. "Hola, *amigo*," she greeted, as the sunshine came in with the opening of the door. She then added, "*Listo para* (Ready for) snorkeling?"

Tina's large smile and sexy body took away the pain from my knee. I grinned back at her. "Yes, I'm ready for a crazy day of water sports, just give me a second to put on my swim trunks, grab a towel and my wetsuit. I'll be out in a second, still need to brush my teeth real quick."

"Better hurry, everyone is waiting on the bus," she said as I closed the door.

Within two minutes I was on the bus and we were heading to the marina. My eyes caught Barbie's as soon as I had climbed all three steps of the bus, searching for a seat. Barbie gave me the evil eye and so did her *amiga*, Jenny.

"Shit, what was this all about?" I scanned my memory bank to solve the riddle of why I was in deep *caca* (shit). "Maybe it was because I took an early exit at the bonfire or because I had gone swimming and left Barbie alone on the beach," I thought to myself. "Or could it be because Barbie had seen me leave with Tina?" My head was spinning from the previous night's libations and searching for quick explanations without firm clues. I didn't have a what, where, who, how or why.

I settled into a seat by myself at the very front and tried to look out the window. I didn't wish to draw any further attention.

"Has anyone seen your roommates?" Matz posed the question loudly so I could not ignore it.

Before I could respond, the daughter of the man who had driven Paul and Marcus to the hospital in Hermosillo said in a rough tone directed at me, "Yeah, my Dad's still not back and he's going to miss scuba diving today. He loves diving."

I turned around to face what I felt was steadily building to form an angry mob. I was getting the persecuted treatment that was given years ago in Salem, Massachusetts to "witches." "I haven't seen or heard anything, but I'm sure they'll all show up soon. Why don't we leave a note and let them know where we are?" I suggested.

"Already done that, Einstein!" Daddy's Girl hissed.

"Excuse me, I don't think we've been introduced," I said in a smart aleck manner, while rising from my seat with my right hand extended as if wanting to shake hands. I made my way back to this girl, who was in the middle of a hissy fit, and confronted her. "I'm Rhet Austen, pleased to meet you."

Her friend who had ridden down with this angry girl tried to separate herself from the closeness of the two sharing the seat. I could tell she didn't want to be involved in this or any words that were about to be tossed around.

She who had made the Einstein comment glared at me. "I know who you are, you're the ex-football player who lost the U of I game for us, and you weren't even in the game."

Before I could say another word, Tina broke in. "Hey, hey that's enough. Shelley is just upset her dad isn't here."

I solemnly apologized to Shelley and waited a few seconds for a reply or an, "I'm sorry, too." Nothing of the sort came from her lips. I turned to the front of the bus and went back to my seat, thinking, "At least I know the bitch's name."

Settling back into my seat, I looked up into the driver's mirror. In the reflective glass I saw Craig's face gleaming with a smile from ear to ear. He seemed to be very pleased with the way things were working against me.

I glared at him and he diverted his eyes back to the road.

Within a few minutes we were at the marina. There waiting for us were employees of Gary's Dive Shop, ready to help us get onto the correct boat. Everyone enthusiastically jumped from their seats and deboarded. I sat in my seat and waited until all the others were off the bus, including Craig—the bus driver and dive master.

Waiting slightly away from the last step was Tina. "C'mon, slowpoke," she kidded, then added, "Do you think you're on Mexican time?"

This drew a grin from me, and I touched her face gently on the cheek. "Thanks for being here on this trip," I said, then added, "I really mean it."

My Bad Tequila

We boarded the boat with the "Snorkelers Here" sign held by a young Mexican man in his early twenties. He was wearing cutoff jeans and a cheap, thin T-shirt with a shark on the back and the words written below, "San Carlos, Mexico." The boat was old and had been painted using two colors, a red that was slightly on the pink side and a sickly, fever-looking yellow.

Looking around the boat, I realized how fortunate I was to be a snorkeler and not a diver on this particular trip. Jenny, Barbie, Shelley, her friend Tracey, and Craig were not boarding the same water vessel as Tina and I. Relief from five sneering, unfriendly looks and remarks were mine for approximately seven hours.

Our boat pulled from the marina first, as we did not have to count tanks and wait for more tanks to be loaded onto the dive boat. The marina was fair sized, with docks marked in alphabetical order from A to M, each with a marine name. Dock A was Albacore, dock D was Dorado, dock J was Jellyfish (I didn't want any part of that dock), and so on and so on. Each dock supported approximately 20 to 25 boats on each side for a total of about 40 or 50 odd boats. Multiply 40 times 13 (the number of letters A–M) and this marina had a capacity of about 500 boats. The larger yachts were tied down on the ends of the docks.

San Carlos's harbor is well protected; it is in an enclosure surrounded 275 degrees by land and mountains. The diesel engine boat we climbed onto coughed black smoke when our captain, Miguel, turned the starting switch hard to the right. A few sputters and the engine settled into a melodic drone. Suddenly we felt the jolt of the boat kick into reverse, nearly sending me into the oil-, gasoline-, and diesel-drenched waters of the marina, as I had not yet planted myself next to Tina. Just as I caught my balance, the antiquish, baby ship hopped into gear, this time sending me sliding on the wooden deck into the captain's legs, knocking the mug from his grease-stained hands. The reason I came in contact with his legs is that the captain's area was built up higher than where we were placed. It resembled a soapbox of sorts, most likely for better vision of the sea and oncoming boats.

"I'm sorry," I managed, as I started to place my sea legs (one supported with a brace) beneath me.

Captain Miguel didn't seem to mind losing his morning coffee; he just grunted and waved it off. "Must happen quite a bit," I tried to convince myself.

After that display of clumsiness, I quickly found a spot and sat on the long, wooden bench next to Tina. There were two benches, one on each side of the boat, that ran approximately six feet, starting about three feet from the rear of the boat. The steering mechanism and throttle were just a little more than right of center. There were stairs leading down into the guts of the boat with a bathroom and a large bed covered with a couple of fishing poles and some tackle. Off to one side was a table with a bench seat. Nothing fancy, but it was functional. On the left-hand side was a step up that would extend around to the front of the boat. The boat was surrounded by an aluminum handrail used as a guide from the step area all the way around to the other side. A person could sit or lay down on the bow if he or she wished to do so.

Tina found my bouncing around the mini ship quite entertaining, as I heard a giggle or two from her. The others were already busy getting soft drinks and water from their coolers and hadn't seemed to notice my fumbling and stumbling. Matz and Ritchie were on this snorkeling expedition, as were two of the chaperones and three other students that seemed to know each other. One of the chaperones, Virginia, was a roommate of Tina and Mindy, and she was also Matz's mother; I did not find out the latter until that morning on the boat ride when I heard Matz slip and mistakenly call her Mom. Prior to that morning he had always referred to her as Virginia.

Our destination, Isla de San Pedro, was approximately 20 to 25 miles to the north of us and we had been told we would see seals—lots of seals.

As our snorkeling ferry chugged from the no-wake area and into the dark open waters I looked at the magnificent homes that surrounded the bay and daydreamed of what it must be to live in such an environment with sun and sea a constant.

"Well, I'm going to the front of the boat to get some sun," Tina said. "Wanna go with me?"

"Sure, I could use a nap," I said as I winked at her, although I don't think she could see it through my dark sunglasses.

Tina led the way and just as I was about to follow, I felt my stomach wrenching and pulling in different directions. "Oh no," I thought, "here we go again."

I went immediately to the rear of the boat, dropped to my knees, positioned myself strongly against the frame of the boat and leaned forward, neck and head outside the boat, and vomited. My stomach heaved until no more fluids came forth, then the dry heaves for a couple more minutes, then tranquility.

I turned to get up off my knees and wipe my mouth and all eyes again upon me. I heard a couple of "ews" and "yucks," but didn't care. I went to the cooler, grabbed a water, finished it in 2.2 seconds, then went down to the head and washed up.

Climbing back up the stairs to the open air, I felt much better and went to join Tina on the bow. She looked at me and said, "You warned me that you may get sick, but I really didn't think it would happen. I thought you were kidding."

"Why would I kid about throwing up?" I responded, as I gave her a slight nudge.

She then leaned over and gave me a kiss on the lips that had just puked. Man, I felt much better already.

We had just spread out our towels and gotten comfortable on the bow of the boat when someone yelled, "Dolphins!"

The small bottlenose dolphins were everywhere circling us, doing tricks, racing from side to side in front of the boat. There had to be at least 100 of them showing us their acrobatic maneuvers. It was an incredible show, and believe me, Sea World has nothing on the Sea of Cortez. This display of dolphin mania went on for about 20 minutes, and at the close of the show, the island we were motoring to came into full view.

It would not be much longer before we were in the 80-degree water, seeing the world beneath the sea surface. We arrived at *Isla de San Pedro*, an uninhabited island, about an hour and a half after our departure. I was looking forward to this snorkeling trip since I had heard San Pedro Island is home to a large population of friendly seals who frequently join snorkelers and divers.

We anchored next to the island. Snorkeling gear was ravaged through and decided upon by those of us who did not have our own. I went underneath to the bedroom area in the bow of the boat and slipped into my florescent green wetsuit. I bought it, almost new, at a yard sale for fifteen bucks a couple of years earlier for water skiing. I had just began to water ski competitively in the top amateur division and needed to look the part. All the other competitors had their own high-dollar slalom skis, wetsuits, and gloves. My slalom ski was a nice, lightly used Connelly which I found in a pawn shop for fifty bucks. The black board, green wetsuit and the black, six-dollar ski gloves from McU Sports made for the perfect inexpensive color-coordinated slalom ski outfit.

Tina traveled with her own gear as she had snorkeled with her family all over the globe. Some of the places she mentioned I had never heard of before.

As for snorkeling gear, I had none, as this was my first legitimate snorkeling experience. As kids growing up on the Snake River my brothers and I had used reeds or old PVC pipes from time to time as makeshift snorkels and used our young, strong eyes without masks to allow us to catch channel catfish with our jersey-gloved hands.

While I squeezed into my wetsuit, Tina had sorted through the snorkeling apparatus and selected for me an almost new blue snorkel and mask that looked as if they might have been a pair. Earlier we had given our shoe size to the Mexican helper guy named Fabian and size *diez* (ten) fins were waiting deck side for me to claim.

Splashing was already taking place as a few bodies were now in the water. Sitting on the wooden plank across the back of the boat, just above the propeller, I put on my gear. As instructed by Tina, I spit into

My Bad Tequila

my mask and rubbed the moisture throughout the windows of it, then rinsed it with seawater. I felt a bit out of place with my wetsuit on as everyone else had on only swimsuits. "Oh well, at least a jellyfish is limited to where it can sting me," I reasoned.

Tina had chosen a life vest, but I declined as I knew that in a buoyancy wetsuit mixed with the saltwater I would have no trouble staying on the surface of the water. And I also wanted to dive and did not wish for the vest to keep me afloat in case I saw something interesting down below and wanted to explore.

Visibility was great at this location, averaging around 40 feet. We made our way toward the base of the island. Once there, we heard a splash! from above, followed by a muted "Aarf! Aarf!" We looked up to see a large sea lion, about eight feet in length, on her way down to check out us snorkelers invading her turf.

These were much larger than what I had expected to encounter, since these were giant SEA LIONS, not little playful SEALS! I had envisioned quite a different scene.

The adult sea lions would jump into the water, swim up within a couple of feet of you, look you square in the eyes for a couple of seconds, then zoom away. They would even come up behind you and nip at your fins. I was scared to death as a couple of them bravely bumped into me; I started to panic and swam back towards the boat.

Everyone but me was enjoying this, including Fabian and Miguel, who were yelling, "Dey want to play, dey your *amigos*, dey your *amigos*." It was determined that the sea lions loved my green wetsuit; evidently these lions of the sea are not color blind. After dog paddling around for a bit with my entire head out of the water so as to see the oncoming assaults, I finally became somewhat more relaxed and tolerant of the giant creatures that would not leave me be. The youngsters were also curious but not as brave, so they would just fly by at top speed without stopping to stare. Their agility and speed were impressive. They are as graceful and quick in the water as they are clumsy and slow on land. The sea lions swam with us throughout our snorkeling adventure, occasionally bumping me to get my attention and each time making my heart race. Those sea monsters seemed to have as much fun as we did.

Even though the sea lions were the highlight of the trip, this area offered other treats as well. I spotted an octopus, its body probably a foot across, with its tentacles wrapped around a rock. We also saw a couple of green moray eels with their heads sticking out of crevasses in the rocks. The entire group saw lots of tropical fish of all colors, including Cortez angel fish, parrot fish, and fairy basslets. A huge school of tuna came by and startled both Tina and me. This surprise group caused me to gasp, and this was the only time during the entire trip I swallowed salt water from the Sea of Cortez. A whole new underwater world was there waiting to be explored. I found that day that I loved snorkeling and would plan to do it many times afterwards with Tina by my side, of course.

Later, while Miguel and Fabian were serving up lunch, I asked if I might grab one of the poles lying on the bed and try my luck bottom fishing.

"*Si, si,*" was the go-ahead acknowledgement, and I proceeded to bait my hook with a small piece of a red snapper that Ritchie had shot with his spear gun. Within two minutes I had a puffer fish on the end of my line, hooked rather well. Pictures were taken and the line was cut by Fabian, letting fish, bait, and hook all free. Fabian did let me save the sinker weights by pulling them upward on the line away from the hook and all that it held. Right away I tied another hook into place and tore more of the snapper apart, this time baiting my hook with a large chunk of seafood. I cast again off the bow of the boat and five minutes later I had a tug at the other end of the line. Setting the hook firmly, I began to reel in. To my great surprise and glee, it was a large green moray eel. I shouted out to everyone and no one in particular, "I've got an eel on my line." Before I could get anyone to take a picture of it, Miguel came running up to me and cut my line, while vehemently saying, "*No bueno, no bueno* (no good)." As quickly as I had my eel, it had been disposed of.

"No pictures, damn," I swore aloud and shook my head in

My Bad Tequila

disgust at Miguel. My fishing for the day was over and I handed him back the rod and reel.

After lunch, all of us went back into the open sea and snorkeled for another hour. A few of the sea lions swam back over to bother us, but not as many as before. Most were comfortable basking in the sun on the craggy rocks that made up the island.

We arrived back a few minutes later than the diving boat. We watched our compadres help disembark empty tanks from the boat to the back of a white pickup truck. The empties would be refilled back at the diving center for the next day's dives.

Everyone from the dive boat was in a great mood and each wanted to tell us of their diving experience as much as we wanted to tell our snorkeling stories. We all opted to go into the Marina Cantina to have a drink and retell our adventures.

Craig, our self-proclaimed diving expert from *Le Bois* (city of trees), had told us San Carlos had unlimited visibility and lots of colorful coral reefs. From the stories we heard this was not completely accurate. At the beginning of the day there was disappointment from the other divers. It's not the Caribbean. There's little coral. No huge barrel or tube sponges. No breathtaking walls and canyons. The visibility is limited, ranging on our trip from 25 to 70 feet. If Craig had been a little more honest, there would have been no disappointments and the inexpensive trip would still have sold out. However, there were lots of challenging and fun dive sites with swim-thru, underwater rock formations, some pinnacles, and tremendous marine life. There were even a couple of wreck dives in the area.

On their first dive they went to a site called *"Tres Marias,"* which was about a 30-minute boat ride from the marina. They swam around and through various underwater rock formations, maxing out at about 50 feet, with visibility of about 20 to 25 feet and hardly any current. Water temperature on this and all of the dives was around 78 to 80 degrees Fahrenheit. The first thing they each had noticed after descending was that there were starfish everywhere, each about eight inches across with neon orange coloration.

"Very cool," was the general response. They also spotted numerous bullseye stingrays flying across the sandy bottom. In one spot a kind of stingray freeway was formed, with stingrays speeding in both directions through a channel between the rocks. "Also, very cool and awesome," were the words mostly heard around the table of margaritas and *cervezas*. The Cortez angelfish were abundant, as were parrotfish and purple fans. All in all, it was a nice, albeit unremarkable, dive to start the trip. It gave all the divers a chance to polish their skills after an absence from the water.

The second dive site of the day for the Boise State divers was at "*Isla de San Antonio*," a sharp, craggy pinnacle jutting from the water. As told by Jenny and Barbie, when they had started their way around the pinnacle, they were engulfed by a school of hundreds of jacks that parted to let them swim through. They spotted several more bull eye stingrays along the bottom, most about 10 to 12 inches in diameter. Also seen were puffer fish, tiny wrasses, more angel fish, parrotfish, and other tropicals, as each of the divers explored the rock formations surrounding the pinnacle. Visibility at this site was better, ranging from 30 to 40 feet. The divers bottomed out at about 45 feet but spent most of their time at 25 to 30 feet where the marine life was more plentiful.

As I lazily drank my cerveza I turned to my girl and saw her again for the first time. She was busy chatting with the others about our day's adventure. I watched her intently and began to think about how I had first met the young and beautiful Miss Tina Valentino. Tina was earning her Bachelor of Arts degree in communication with a journalism emphasis, hoping to become a journalist. I was majoring in English literature in hopes of someday becoming a famous author or working as a sports columnist for a medium-sized newspaper, or at the very least, being able to teach English as a Second Language (ESL).

The previous fall semester we had both been enrolled in the same Broadcasting Techniques class and had worked together on a group project. Tina had asked me more than once, "Where have we met?" I told her each time, "Before this class, never." She would always disagree, saying, "We have met once before, I know it."

My Bad Tequila

She then took the small light blue diary that was constantly with her and wrote down some notes. I had once asked about the diary and she had told me her thoughts, her joys, and her sorrows were all in that little book. "It's my life," she said.

There had been some strong animal attraction between us from the beginning, but I had a girlfriend and wisely, neither of us acted on our instincts. But this last spring semester Tina and I found each other again, sharing another subject during the same class period. Communication Theory and Philosophy was the class where we ultimately "hooked up" and became better acquainted.

That first Tuesday, when I had entered class with a cast on my right leg and unskillfully using crutches, Tina had been right there from the start. She helped me through the doorway, and lifted the textbook-laden backpack that was swinging from my shoulder onto a desk. It sided to where her notebook, text, and pen sat atop a neighboring desk.

From that time on, I looked forward to arriving at Room 137 of the Communication Building every Tuesday and Thursday for a full hour and thirty minutes. The very first day of class we became "study buddies" and grew to know and understand each other more every session. In the beginning we met at the library, then the student lounge, then progressed to meet for lunch or coffee. Eventually, we didn't even open our texts or notebooks at these meetings, we just talked. We talked about our families, about growing up, about what we liked and what we didn't like. Sometimes it seemed as if we didn't talk about anything in particular but still the hours cruised by. On more than one occasion Tina would open her diary, jot down a quick entry, and the book would once again close.

Our first date had been fun and had turned into an all-nighter. I picked Tina up at her apartment to see "Top Gun." Tom Cruise played Maverick, the macho student ace pilot. Kelly McGillis was Charlie, one of the flight instructors, and Val Kilmer was Iceman, the nemesis of Maverick, just as cocky a student and just as daring but more prickish and not as likable as Mr. Cruise. And then there was

Goose, Maverick's playful partner and best friend, whose untimely death adds realism to the film. Goose (Anthony Edwards) left behind a beautiful young widow named Carole (Meg Ryan), who uttered the famous movie quote, "Take me to bed or lose me forever." This all-star film was the top grossing movie of 1986 and instantly considered a classic.

My movie choice was perfect; afterwards we had a sandwich at Cobby's Sandwich Shop in Boise near the stadium. The reason I had chosen this place was twofold: first, Cobby's sandwiches are second to none. Second, I was working part time at Cobby's first location so my meal was free and Tina's would be nearly free. Not that I'm a cheapskate, but the food is great, and I wanted her to know a little more about me and my life.

I had recommended Tina to order either the number 15 or number 23. Both were my favorite, the 15 consisted of *Capicollo, Genoa, Cotto,* and *Mortadella* Italian meats, Mozzarella cheese, tomatoes, lettuce, onions, *pepperoncinis* and mayonnaise on sourdough bread. The 23 was turkey and avocado with swiss cheese and the same vegetables with mayonnaise and sourdough bread. Tina had taken my advice and ordered the turkey and avocado so naturally I ordered the Italian as a little food trading would be in order. It worked out perfectly as per "Rhet's plan," Tina liked them both and had no problem sharing the two tasty sandwiches.

After dinner and a couple of beers, Tina invited me to her apartment near the university. She lived in a one-bedroom, brick fourplex-style apartment. It was cutely decorated with modern deco furniture and a few pictures of family and friends. I found one photo more adorable and interesting than the others. The 8x10 photo, in an expensive-looking silver frame showed Tina, an olive-skinned, handsome young man, and an Irish Setter with the most beautiful rusty colored long hair covering its entire doggie frame. The photograph was taken at the edge of an orchard. Tina was sitting on a rock, and the teenage boy, who looked about the same age as or maybe a little older than Tina, had his arm around her shoulder. The Irish Setter was standing on all fours, tail high in the air. Due to the depth perception of the picture, the tip of its tail touched the full, bright sun to the right of the orchard. I stared at the photograph for nearly 30 seconds, gazing at one of the most beautiful creatures I had laid eyes upon. The dog was incredible, too. "Who is the guy in the picture?" I wondered, just a faint bit jealous. "Old boyfriend?" I questioned, trying to sound as if I could care the least bit.

"No…it's my brother." She lingered for a few seconds before continuing, "It was our last picture together."

No sooner had the words left Tina's soft lips then a salty mist spilled from her bright brown eyes.

"Ohhh, I'm sorry," was all I could muster from my now-very-dry throat. I knew better than to say anything else as I, too, had lost a brother while growing up. After an awkward few seconds, I offered up, still with a parched voice, "I guess I'll be going."

"Please stay," she asked strongly. "That is, if you would like to." "Sure, I'd love to," was my quick and spontaneous answer. No more was said the rest of the evening about the picture, the dog, the brother or anything else personal.

That night Tina had opened a bottle of red merlot and asked if I liked to play Scrabble. I love Scrabble. I had always loved words, English and spelling. Scrabble and Monopoly were two of my favorite board games, and they were Tina's favorites too. Thus, the all-nighter, drinking two bottles of merlot and playing Scrabble until 4:30 a.m. Sunday, then falling asleep with Tina in my arms on the small sofa. Or it might have been a love seat?

This was the beginning of the end with regards to my relationship with Aimee. It had also marked a starting point of my building a new one with Tina.

After that night of Scrabble, I remained at Tina's place other than attending class, work, getting clean clothes from my place, and eating.

Aimee finally had enough of my constant study sessions with my new classmate. I was sure she could feel us gradually moving apart as she concentrated on her accounting degree, and I concentrated on Tina. This last episode of not calling her on Saturday night, nor coming back to her place or phoning until the following Thursday, had pulled the final nail from our relationship. Our bond had been torn apart, the same as a wooden building when all the planks are removed. Oddly, I had helped Aimee's dad tear down an old shed on their farm, pulling out one nail after another, until finally just planks of wood were stacked where once stood a structure.

It was not my intention of having another steady girlfriend in Tina, even though I wanted to be near her all the time. I had mentioned to her about this Spring Break getaway but had not invited her; I was not completely sure where my head was. I had wanted to use this time to contemplate the next step in my life. However, Tina had shown up and I was delighted.

"Uugh," I grunted. I felt a slight jab in my side and felt the ocean mist from a sudden gust of breeze touch my face and my arm that I had now stretched out around Tina. She had poked me in the ribs to get my attention and had asked me a question. No longer was I was in the clouds or on the sea, I was back on land.

"Huh?" I drowsily asked, hoping she did not mind repeating herself.

Tina again asked, "What are you daydreaming about?"

"Nothing in particular," I lied as I had missed some of the conversation thinking about Tina's and my short but already significant past. I raised my glass in the air, toward the center of the table and our crowd, profoundly stating, "*Salud*, Craig, for a great trip." Everyone raised his and her glass and or bottle and in unison toasted, "*Salud*, Craig."

After a couple more rounds of *bebidas* (drinks), we joyfully (due to a buzz) boarded the long blue vehicle with the BSU lettering and the portrait of a horse etched on each side. We probably would have lingered for at least two more beers or margaritas, but Shelley had prodded us along. She reminded us we needed to get back to our boarding bunks as her dad and the others would be waiting for us, back

My Bad Tequila

from the Hermosillo hospital.
    A short bus ride later we were back at the Gringo Hotel.

CHAPTER 7

Theodore's Return
(Regresa de Theodore)

The thing we all noticed first was Teddy standing alone in the parking lot with a cast on his wrist and lower arm. No Suburban, no Papa for Shelley, no Paul, and no Marcus. Just like that, the mood changed from joyful to puzzled and concerned. My immediate thought was, "Oh shit, where is daddy-o and that Suburban?"

Again, I stayed on the bus until it cleared of the other riders as I was not in a rush to question Teddy, nor in a rush to hear his response. The bus cleared in record time and Teddy was instantly surrounded as if he had just scored the winning touchdown at a homecoming game or pitched a near perfect game with a one hitter to win the championship.

"Where's my dad?" was the question I heard above all other

inquiries.

Teddy looked confused, sounded confused, and I believe he was truly confused. "What, what are you talking about?" "Where's Paul, where is Marcus?" His responses to questions were questions, and he posed more questions than anyone fired at him.

After several minutes of a complete clusterfuck, things still were not sorted out. Teddy had not seen nor heard from anyone since being loaded on the stretcher and into the ambulance at Club Med. He had been put on a Mexican tour bus similar to a Trailways or Greyhound bus in the United States. The English-speaking Mexican doctor who had treated him and set his wrist last night had driven Teddy to the bus station and somehow managed to get him a much-discounted fare to Guaymas. After arriving in Guaymas in the early morning at the busy bus terminal in the middle of town, Teddy had finally located the correct local bus and stop in Guaymas that went into San Carlos and dropped off the locals for work. He had disembarked at the stop nearest the hotel and walked up the hill and to his room.

We must have just missed him by an hour or so, as Teddy informed us he arrived at the hotel around 10 a.m. that morning. He had spent most of the day waiting and walking aimlessly around the hotel complex, which would have had him covering his footsteps continuously due to the small piece of acreage.

Still the questions were out there, each by itself, as lonely as a streaker on the 35-yard line at a football game. "Where were the others?" "Where had they gone, if they had not shown up at the hospital?" "Was there more than just the one hospital where Teddy had been treated?" "What now?" These were the questions I had in my head, the same ones were being asked aloud by others, most particularly by Shelley.

Not being able to bear the repeated questions any longer, I retreated to my room. At least one of my new bunkmates was safe and home. I went straight to my cot, tossed off my flip flops, pulled my shirt up over my head, and flopped my salty flesh onto the bed. There had to be some logical reason why the Suburban and its cargo had not yet returned, but without any new thoughts or theories I was stumped.

Drifting off into a slumber, I dreamed I was alone on a wooden raft at sea during a tremendous and ominous storm. Teddy's voice awakened me and then I was back, safely on land.

"Rhet, are you awake?" "Yes, Teddy, I'm awake," I spoke in an anxious and thankful tone.

This was one of the few times I did not mind being drawn from slumber after having a couple of cocktails. I didn't want to find out what would have happened in my nightmare.

I sat up on the bed and Teddy sat down next to me. "Where do you think my friends are?" His voice sounded like a child asking his mother where his favorite toy had gone.

Teddy looked terrible. He was pale and sickly looking, and his eyes were too far back in his head.

"Theodore, have you eaten anything today?" My voice was more accusatory than questioning. This was not the time to call him Teddy.

"I don't think I have. No, I guess not," was his weak reply.

Quickly I pulled my shirt back over my head, slipped my big toes into place around the thongs of the flip flops, and gently grabbed Teddy's arm. "Let's go and grab a taco or something," I said, and we left the drab room.

I wanted to see if Tina wished to accompany us but I did not want to take a chance of running into any of the other girls since their rooms were so close; so I opted for us to walk directly to the office. Luis was there, loyal and ready for customers and their requests. He offered to drop us off at Barracuda Bob's near the marina for a quick bite as he needed to grab some vegetables and tortillas in town. I believe Luis also could see Teddy needed some food and he needed it as quickly as possible. But it was late in the afternoon and Barracuda Bob's had closed for the day. Luis told us he knew of another place for good Mexican food.

He dropped us off at Rosa's Cantina, a small restaurant with roses and vines painted on the exterior walls. We each had a Mexican

My Bad Tequila

plate, with two *carne asada* (roasted beef) tacos, rice, refried beans and a tortilla. I had a beer and Teddy chased his meal with a Coca Cola.

Color returned to Teddy's skin and his eyes now looked like they actually fit in their sockets. I picked up *la cuenta* (the tab), though my guilt still had not been satisfied.

We walked back to the Gringo Hotel without saying much. I believe Teddy was missing his buddies and I wanted them here nearly as badly. I just wanted to live and let live. I just wanted everyone together again on this trip, with everyone having an outstanding vacation with no more bickering amongst the group.

I did mention to Teddy at the end of our walk that Tina and I were going out for the evening to do some drinking, listening to music, and dancing. I told him it would be great if he could join us and assured him that Paul and Marcus would be back anytime. "They most likely went to the wrong hospital and are on their way back here," I said. "I bet they'll show any minute. We'll leave in about an hour, and if they still haven't shown, we'll leave them a note." I then added, "Tina heard about a fun place. Maybe some of the other girls might want to tag along."

Teddy showed a little more life at this last suggestion, as I am close to certain his status was still innocent (aka virgin. He continued walking to our room as I stopped outside Tina's threshold and knocked on the door.

"Who is it?" Virginia called out.

"I'm here to see Tina, please," my voice struggling and a bit tense. "Coming," I heard Tina say, and an instant later she opened the door and stepped into the evening air with me.

"Hey, *chica*, where were you thinking we should go tonight?"

Before she could answer, I added, "I invited Teddy, I hope that's okay."

"Of course!!, I think that's awesome of you to ask Teddy, especially with his friends still not back."

"Do you think any of the other girls would care to go?" I threaded the question carefully so as not to prick myself with the needle.

"I'll ask." Tina hesitated and then added, "Anyone in particular I should invite?"

"How about Mindy? Unless she has been lassoed into Craig's corral and has plans," I suggested.

Tina headed back to her stoop and asked, "What time are we going?"

"I told Teddy in about an hour. Oh, and before I forget, let's call him Theodore tonight so as not to upset him any further."

"See you in an hour." Tina gave a quick smile and was back inside her room.

I turned to go cleanup for the evening and remembered what I had set out to do. I did a 180-degree turn and again tapped on the girl's door.

"Tina, I need to ask you a quick question," I bellowed through the thin door.

No sooner had I finished my sentence than Tina was there. "Yes?" she said, as she stood leaning against the entrance.

"Where are we going? I need to tell Teddy so he can leave a note for his *amigos*."

"Buccaneers. It's a palapa bar in the middle of San Carlos headed towards Guaymas. It's supposed to be a lot of fun and great *musica*." "*Excellente*," I replied in the Spanish language and gave her a quick hug. "*Adios, amiga*," and Tina disappeared.

Entering my room, I noticed Teddy looking at all the scuba gear, which included three individual sets of unused equipment. The regulators, fins, and all other apparatus had traveled in a bus 1500 miles and now lay motionless in a drab Mexican hotel.

Wanting to lift his mood, I tried to put excitement into my voice as I said, "Tina's gonna see if Mindy wants to join us. You look great in that Hawaiian shirt."

Seventy minutes later the two of us were at Tina's door. At the first knock, Tina and Mindy were surprisingly on time and joining us outside. Both girls looked great and I could see Teddy was pleased. I'm

My Bad Tequila

sure Mindy was looking forward to the evening away from "Mr. Diver." Earlier that day at our rendezvous point at Marina Cantina, Craig had made sure to grab the chair nearest Mindy and sat as close as the chairs had allowed.

The four of us made our way to the bus stop, waiting no more than 10 minutes for a partially crowded gray bus that had once been white, with the header Guaymas in the window. I gave a 10-*peso* coin to the driver and he gave me a two-*peso* piece back in change; he tossed the other coin in the bus fare coin depositor. Ten minutes later we were walking into Buccaneers.

Music greeted us as we stepped into the large *palapa* structure. Van Halen's 1986 hit album, "5150," was playing. It was the band's first number one album on the Billboard charts, driven by the keyboard-dominated single "Why Can't This Be Love" sung by Sammy Hagar.

We found a table in the center of the bar and restaurant. Immediately I grabbed Tina's hand and we walked to the dance floor and swayed to the lyrics and music of Sammy, the Red Rocker.

Teddy and Mindy went to the bar, brought back four Pacifico beers, and waited for us to clear the dance floor. There was a large pirate statue that looked a bit like Captain Morgan on the namesake bottle of rum. I yelled to Teddy and Mindy, "Look at the giant pirate."

"He is a buccaneer, not a pirate," Mindy said.

"Whatever." I rolled my eyes jokingly.

She then responded playfully, "Please respect the name of the establishment, 'The Buccaneer.'"

"Does anyone know why Van Halen named their seventh album "5150?" I asked. Tina knew the answer and I was again falling fast for her. She was my kind of chick, a girl who loved Sammy Hagar and knew about Van Halen.

"Van Halen named their album '5150' because that's the section of the California Welfare and Institutions Code which allows a qualified officer or clinician to involuntarily confine someone with a mental disorder that makes him a danger to himself," Tina explained.

Mindy chimed in. "Now I get why all the band members were in straitjackets in the photo on the inside cover of that album."

Teddy looked confused and I knew he must not follow hard rock. Whether he liked it or not, I do not know, nor did I wish to ask anything that might make him uncomfortable this particular night.

After this album ended, tunes from the Beach Boys started up. "California Girls" was being harmonized by the famous California boy band of yesteryear. At the end of the song I asked the group if they wanted to hear a cool true story about my chance encounter with the Beach Boys.

All three said they did.

"Well, let's see, it was the summer of 1982 in Boise. I bicycled down to the Red Lion Inn just off the greenbelt to swim in the pool, hang out, and work on my tan. I had done this several times that year and the year before. I knew Jewels the bartender because we had gone out a couple of times for drinks, etcetera, etcetera."

Tina broke in. "What is etcetera, etcetera?" she teased.

"I think you know what that is! May I continue?" I asked, with my best boyish grin.

"As I was saying, I would usually have a drink or two poolside, swim some laps, and leave a decent gratuity. Basically, I minded my own business and added to the ambience of the pool scenery." I paused and winked at Tina.

"Anyway, the Beach Boys were in town for a concert the night before and I wanted to go but had to work that evening. That next morning I pedaled down to the Red Lion Inn. I'm in the pool area and there are the Beach Boys, just hanging at the pool. I can't stand it as I know each of them by face from the albums I had won from KFXD radio station the summer before. I walk up to the table to where the group is and boldly declare, 'You guys are the Beach Boys aren't you!'

"Al Jardine then says, 'You must not have gone to our concert last night or you would have known we were staying here. We announced to the crowd where we were staying in case any of them wanted to join us in the night club later on. We usually don't let anyone know where we are staying, but the crowd was so into the show and into us, that we really wanted to meet some of our true fans.'

"'I wanted to go to your concert,' I said, 'but had to work, driving a dump truck from four to midnight. I asked my boss for the evening off, but he wouldn't let me have it. I have eight of your albums. If I run home real quick and grab them, will you guys sign them?'

"Mike Love responded, half believing my sincerity of having their albums, 'Yeah, if you can get them here within the hour, we'll sign them.'"

"'Thanks, and I'll be right back,' I yelled over my shoulder as I ran to the parking lot to loosen my bicycle from its chain.

"Twenty-five minutes later, sweat dripping from my forehead, I returned with eight of their albums and a red marker for signature signing, all in a wrinkled plastic bag.

"When I handed the albums over to Al Jardine, he instantly became concerned and called the rest of the band over. 'You guys need to see these albums; we've never had these approved.' Mr. Jardine turned to me and accusingly asked, 'Where did you get these albums?'

"I started to stutter. 'I, I won them from the radio station here in town last summer.'

"Mike Love then took over the questioning. 'What radio station and how?'

"'KFXD, 101.9,' I responded as quickly as possible, hoping to end this band-on-fan interrogation session. 'I called in, tenth caller, won the albums, then I qualified for the grand prize of my own private beach party with nine of my friends. I won the grand prize as well, but to me the grand prize were your albums.' I looked at each member, pleading forgiveness for whatever wrong I had committed against this band and their record label.

"Mike Love could tell from my nervousness, I was wishing that I had not come to the Red Lion pool that day, thus escaping my chance to meet with the Beach Boys. He eased off.

"'What's your name, son?' he asked with a grin.

"'Rhet, Rhet Austen,' I replied as I extended my hand. 'Pleased to meet you, Mr. Love.'

"'Call me Mike,' he said reassuringly. 'Don't worry, you haven't done anything wrong,' he added, and he took the felt marker from my unstable hand and started signing my albums, all eight of them.

"Al Jardine then took the marker, introduced himself and the other band members, and signed three of the albums for me, as did Brian Wilson and Bruce Johnston.

"Al then called over his two sons, who were spending part of the summer with their dad while he was touring. I can't recall their names but the oldest was fifteen at the time and the other was about nine or ten.

"The group told me what their concerns were with the 'never seen before albums.' As a band, they had never received any royalties for these album remakes, all the albums claimed to be by Capitol Records as a Capitol Re-issue and five of the albums had a disclaimer 'This album has fewer songs than the original album.' Al and Mike both took notes.

"'Now I understood. It was about money,' I calculated quickly in my mind.

"'The London Telegraph – Beach Boys '69,' 'Spirit of America,' and 'Endless Summer,' were each signed by Al Jardine, Brian Wilson, Mike Love' and Bruce Johnston.

"'California Girls,' 'Surfing USA,' 'Fun Fun Fun,' 'Surfer Girl,' and 'Dance Dance Dance' were all signed individually and solely by Mike Love.

"I was invited to have lunch with them, under a canopy in the open Idaho air, next to the large, sparkling pool. After lunch, they went to their rooms to change clothes and told me they would be back to say goodbye.

"True to their word, all of them came by the pool and asked if I had ever seen a tour bus. Obviously, being a kid from the country, I had never even stepped foot into a motor home, let alone a 40-foot touring coach. We headed to the parking lot through the main foyer

My Bad Tequila

of the hotel like old friends, and then the double doors came busting open from a convention room and we were surrounded by hundreds of screaming girls. Seems the Miss Idaho Pageant was taking place and Miss Counties and Miss Towns and Miss Cities from all over the Great State of Idaho were competing for the coveted crown. Each girl waved pen and paper at the band.

"I just stood there, motionless, mouth agape, when Mike Love yells over to me, 'Rhet, start signing autographs for these girls.' I obeyed and I was briefly a part of the band.

"So, there are girls all over the state of Idaho that have a signature that reads, 'With Love, Rhet Austen.'

"The Boys all made their way to the coach, boarded, and were able to close the doors without any teenage girls climbing on after them. I never did make it onto the bus; I was too busy signing napkins and hotel scratch pads for pretty young girls that I didn't even see the band make its getaway. 'Band on the Run' came to my mind. They were professionals, I was an amateur, and it clearly showed. The bus was pulling away and girls were now confused as to why I was not on the bus. Instinct kicked in and I started running after the bus screaming; 'You left me, wait for me, idiots. Come back, come back.'

"Later that day, I hopped on my bike, went home, turned on the turntable and sang along with the 'World Famous BEACH BOYS.'

"And that my friends, is my Beach Boy story." I finished, then had a long, pleasurable gulp from the dark brown bottle with the yellow lettering that read Pacifico *cerveza*.

"Bravo, that was a great story. I even believe it, because of the detail," Tina said while picking up her beer and offering me a toast.

Mindy added, "Here's to the original Beach Boys and their one day addition, Rhet 'Frankly, my dear, I don't give a damn' Austen."

The four of us all raised our glasses and bellowed, "The Beach Boys."

With my story finished, most of us returned to listening to Jimmy Buffett harmonizing "Margaritaville." The two girls and I sang along, tapping our fingers on the table and our toes and heels on the wooden floor in time with the song that plays on any vacation at any beach in the world.

The exception to the rule of having fun this evening was Teddy.

"He was like a puppy that had been separated from the litter. He was constantly looking for the return of playmates just like a puppy awaiting the return of his brothers or sisters that mysteriously had been taken from the enclosed pen. The big difference between Ted and the puppies was each day the puppies remembered less, and spent less time thinking about their previous companions, all the while becoming more independent. Ted, on the other hand remembered more each hour and his total thought process was engulfed with loneliness as he continued to fall deeper on the need for their presence," I scribbled in my head.

From that day forward, and to this day, I no longer think of the common phrase "puppy love." I think of "Teddy love" when I see a lonesome soul, pining away for lost *amigos*, loves, or companions.

Tina walked to the bar and brought back a Diet Coke, giving me the rest of her beer. It didn't taste at all good to her, she said. I finished her beer upon completion of my own, then downed another and another while getting lost in the unbelievable tunes being played.

Under the thatched roof, Tina and I dirty danced most of the night, (even though "Dirty Dancing" and Patrick Swayze were not a household name at that time, young people still knew what it was to grind.) The three of us signed Teddy's cast before he caught a bus ride back in the direction of the hotel. Mindy took turns dancing with Tina, me and others in the bar, including Tina's three friends who had given us a ride to Club Med the evening before. This time they had an *amiga* with them. She was about the same age as the others and was pretty but not dazzling. Daniella was her name and she seemed quiet, although she did seem more comfortable when conversing with Tina in the romance language of Spanish.

With the alcohol flowing freely, many of the other patrons including some vacationing Americans; some vacationing Canadians;

My Bad Tequila

some vacationing Mexicans; and some locals of all three nationalities began dancing on the bar. The slick wooden bar had *peso* pieces beneath a glass top. There were ten-*peso* coins, five-*peso* coins, two-*peso* coins and one-*peso* coins spread throughout the 30-foot length of bar. I started to wonder out how many *pesos* were under the glass and what it would calculate to in American dollars, but instead climbed onto a stool and joined the other revelers on top of the long, wide, wooden plank with no sea below. The bar top is made for interesting dancing and balance-keeping. It was smooth and slick in some areas and damn right sticky in others.

With little convincing, Tina and Mindy were on the bar on either side of me, shaking their stuff and splashing spilt beer, rum, tequila, whiskey, vodka, soda pop, lime juice and tonic water up into their sandals. Juan, too, joined us, leaving Mamo, Victor and Daniella on the safe ground below. Becoming braver all the time, I decided to try a rather difficult dismount onto a stool approximately five feet away from the platform on which we all stood. Technically, it was a great leap from the bar to the stool, the landing not as technical as I tried to emulate John Wayne jumping into the saddle on his horse. I stuck my landing on the stool, but my inner thighs paid dearly for their bareness as slivers ran deep into my flesh and a blood vessel busted on my left thigh. From my vantage point up top, the stools appeared as if normal finishes and sanding had been taken care of, but they had not. My knee came away unscathed, but my face should have been slapped doubly hard for the stupidity.

After taking my leap of idiocy, I spun around to face the revelers on the bar and saw Juan snuggling closer to Tina. Instant anger overcame me, anger at myself for taking the ill-advised plunge and for leaving my gal dancing on the bar with a guy I didn't know and sure as hell didn't trust him as far as an empty beer bottle throw away. The guy definitely wanted Tina and could tell her so in a beautiful accent and language Tina enjoyed listening to and responding to. She could use the same sexy accent that seemed to come natural to her to converse with him. My English vocabulary might be larger but my Spanish was much smaller than the other fella's.

The song ended and I rose quickly to help bring Tina back to the ground and away from the other guy.

Shortly after, I was ready for a departing shot of tequila and a ride to our sleeping quarters where I could be alone with Tina. Mindy, Tina, and I hopped into a taxi; Juan had offered us a ride, but we told him and the others to stay and enjoy themselves. This was one of the few times I was glad to pick up the entire cost of the ride.

Tina was safe with me and I with her; we held hands the entire trip back to the hotel. If Mindy had not been with us, more than hands would have been held.

A short taxi ride later the three *amigos* were exiting the taxi, I a little slower than the two *amigas* due to the wooden spikes still under my skin like blood leaches. We had dug and pulled out the obvious ones at the "Pirate Place," but many others still ached to be yanked out.

All three of us were looking for the same thing, a Suburban that was not there. "Damn," I swore to myself.

I walked Tina and Mindy to their rooms and gave Mindy a hug with a sign off of, "See ya tomorrow, *amiga*."

Tina did the same and Mindy left us alone in the night. One eve away from a full moon, everything was well lit. We looked down at the marina and could see the reflection of the moon skimming off the water. Absolutely magnificent, the water resembled a perfectly flat mirror reflecting the moon's face back to itself. Our hands still loved holding their new friends and our fingers enjoyed exploring the other's hands. We held one another tightly and began to kiss uncontrollably and recklessly.

I realized, or started to think I loved Tina, and I had the same feeling that she loved me too.

Separating just long enough to make our way back to the hotel, I quietly took the key and string from around my neck and unlocked our door. How I wished there were three roommates we did not want to wake, instead of just the lone Teddy.

My Bad Tequila

Moonlight streamed in through the bathroom, and for the first time I noticed pale corrugated fiberglass above the toilet. I asked Tina if her bathroom had it, but she just put an index finger to lips and said, "shh."

Seeing all the scuba gear in the room reminded us of our missing party. We looked at Teddy's bunk and he seemed to be asleep, but very restless. He kept mumbling and rocking from shoulder to shoulder.

I led the way to my cot in the corner and pulled back the sheet and blanket for Tina to make her way into my bed. She had her shorts and tank top off and had crawled onto the narrow bed before I could get my brace off.

A sharp pain reminded me of the splinters still in both legs so I made my way to the bathroom, rummaged for a pair of tweezers in my shaving kit, placed myself on the toilet and began "operation slivers."

Ten minutes later I was crawling into bed and snuggling up against Tina's warm, naked body. I still had on my boxer shorts but my hard and nearly fully erect member had found its way through the opening and pressed against Tina's soft skin. We began kissing furiously, briefly forgetting the other person in the tiny room.

Touching a woman had never felt more real for me than it did at this moment. My mouth and tongue left her neck and face and found their way to Tina's soft breasts.

I wanted to and would make love to this young woman who was so full of life and voluptuous. Tina pulled me closer, I quickly removed my underwear, giving them a heave onto the Saltillo-tiled floor.

Immediately I climbed onto Tina and found my way into her body. We both tried intently to get closer. I tried to push deeper and she tried to pull me further into her. Passionately and quietly we made love until we both were spent. I continued kissing Tina's neck and face as our hips slowed and finally came to a complete halt. I kissed her once more, long and hard on the mouth, and exited her beautiful body, rolling to my left and away from the wall.

Tina found my shirt and tiptoed to use the bathroom.

Teddy was still tossing and grumbling. We had not awakened him. I drifted off to sleep momentarily but was instantly awake when Tina was at the foot of the bed, trying to climb back into our small love cot. We held each other. I told her I loved her and she whispered back that she loved me. Life at that moment, in Mexico, was *perfecto* (perfect).

My Bad Tequila

Rico's Beach Boys albums all signed by Mike Love at the Red Lion Inn - Boise, ID

CHAPTER 8

The Decision
(La Decision)

The next morning, I awoke to find Teddy standing over my bed. "Rhet, I need to talk with you, are you awake?" "Still no word from Marcus and Paul?" I replied, half questioning, half stating while trying to cover my wide yawn with my right hand. "What are we going to do?" he begged, trying to ignore my bed companion, the top half of her body in plain view.

I quickly pulled at the lone sheet and covered Tina, who was now stirring at hearing the distant sound of voices entering her head closer and louder.

"Relax, Teddy," I said and tried to ease his anxiety. "Let's go down to visit Luis, I remember seeing a telephone on the counter. We'll call the hospital where you were treated, to see if they've seen our gang. They're probably just lost or maybe had car trouble. Don't

My Bad Tequila

worry, we'll find them and then we'll go fishing today. My treat," I added with my best positive-sounding voice.

I told Teddy I'd meet him outside in a few minutes, hinting that I was without underwear and did not want to put another weird moment into our short history.

I spotted Tina's diary lying on the tile, looked at her with her eyes still shut, and grabbed it up. I thought about opening it, then ruled against it, and laid the diary on the bed next to the sleeping beauty.

Kissing Tina good morning and goodbye for the time being, I made my way into the shower and was out in the bright sunlight within eight minutes. Teddy and I walked down to the office but the phone was unavailable. "*No funciario*" was the explanation given by hotel management.

Luis did tell us about the Marina Terra, a resort hotel next to the marina where telephone service was available. He also told us that two of the girls in our group were looking for a telephone as well.

"Shit," I said. "What?" asked Teddy.

"*Que?*" was the form that Luis's same question came as.

"Oh, it's just that the girls are going to be there and if Shelley is one of them, I know she is going to direct her anger toward me," I answered.

Teddy nodded his head in acknowledgement, and Luis nodded as well but not with the same complete understanding.

We hiked to the Marina Terra resort hotel without any further words, other than my asking, "Ted, you don't blame me, do you?"

Teddy couldn't fight back the tears and seeing his, neither could I. "Rhet, I, I just want to see my friends, that's all I care about."

"I know, and I'm sorry for everything," I said as I wiped the moisture from my eyes with the bottom of my bright blue Hawaiian shirt. Upon reaching the hotel we did indeed see Shelley, her best friend, and Craig talking with the receptionist and pointing at the black telephone sitting on a desk behind the counter.

I slowed to a complete stop as I did not wish to encounter any of them. Teddy kept his pace and greeted them. My distance kept me from hearing the conversation, but I had a good idea what was being verbalized, as the threesome had spotted me standing at the top of the stairs. I stood motionless as a cottontail bunny in the open desert, hoping to stay hidden from the preying coyotes. I, like the soon-to-be-dead bunny, did not twitch.

After standing alone for a few seconds I decided to check out the hotel and walked through the lobby, pretending to look at the art on the walls.

Quietly I slipped out the double glass doors at the opposite end of the entry way. It looked as if Edward Scissorhands lived nearby (although at that time the character had not been created). Medium-sized trees and large, hearty bushes were trimmed in the shape of Mexican men, complete with sombreros and mustaches. There were trees shaped like square-framed houses with connecting fireplaces alongside. One large bush resembled a giant chicken, another resembled a rabbit, and still another, a whale.

I forgot my troubles for an instant and made my way down a few steps to stroll through this man-made garden. Wandering along the sidewalk I eventually stumbled onto the pool area complete with a bar, waiters, and a blaring stereo. The resort's pool was a few steps above a restaurant and the entire lower marina showcased all the yachts nearby.

Not wanting to pass the bar without getting a cool beverage, I ordered a *piña coloda*. It was served in a plastic cup in less than five minutes, topped with some nutmeg and garnished with a bright red cherry with a bent brown stem. It was still early, but I needed this drink badly, for I knew that eventually I would need to go back into the hotel lobby to meet Teddy. Most likely the rest of the motley fricking crew would be there as well.

Entering the lobby with two thirds of my *piña coloda* already gone, I was delighted to find only Teddy sitting on a half-circular black leather couch facing the television and half-watching a daytime *novela* (soap opera).

I sat down next to Teddy and asked, "Any news from the

My Bad Tequila

hospital?" Teddy's expression said it all.

"Nothing?" I asked, before I had time to think about what reply I might receive, now that Teddy didn't seem so much like a cuddly stuffed animal.

"Nothing. Absolutely, fucking nothing." There was contempt in his voice, but the harsh statement was followed by a stream of salty tears running down his freckled face.

Not knowing if I should seek more information, I finally asked, "Who spoke with the hospital?"

"That lady there." He pointed in the direction of the front desk where a young lady and middle-aged man were engrossed in conversation. She translated what we told her to the hospital administrator over the telephone. Not one person recollects seeing them there, but several people remember me being brought in by ambulance two nights ago."

I hated asking the next question; but if I didn't I knew my mind would torment me. "Did she ask if anyone else was admitted that night, ah, perhaps from an accident?"

"Yes, Shelley asked her to translate that question for us, and the nurse, or whoever the lady was speaking to at the hospital, said there was another young man 18 to 23 years old brought by ambulance that night. He did not have any ID on him and was unconscious. No one else, no other emergencies, nothing."

"Was the guy American or Mexican?" I dug deeper into the uncharted waters of Teddy's temperament.

"She didn't know. But what difference does it make? It's not Marcus or Paul—it was only one person, they are three."

"Damn...where could they have gone?" I was questioning myself more than asking Teddy for an answer.

Teddy's crying had left his face red, wet, and partly swollen, and now his nose was starting to drip. I jumped up off the couch and hustled to the men's bathroom to get Teddy several paper towels.

"Thanks Rhet," he said. This was at least a relief. Teddy was back to being a nice kid and not the jackass he seemed to be a couple of minutes earlier.

"Teddy—sorry, I mean Theodore." I mentally kicked myself as I ignorantly misstated his name in his presence. Continuing on, I spoke with little conviction. "I honestly don't know what to do or say. I have no clues as to what we should do or where we would even start to look for them."

"Did Shelley call home to her mother?" I asked suddenly.

"Yes, and her mother has not heard one word. Now she is worried and frantic as well."

"There has to be some explanation, but I don't know what it is!" I exclaimed. "Let's walk back to the room and find out what the gang wants to do." Off we strode, both of us straining our eyes each time we heard or saw a vehicle approach in hopes that it was Teddy's *amigos*.

As we turned the corner after walking up the hill, everyone except the missing was in a closed circle and appeared to be having a meeting of sorts.

Tina eyed us right away and waved for us to hurry over.

Within seconds Ted and I were a part of this growing imperfect circle. Craig was the first to speak. "Theodore, Rhet, we are taking a vote on returning to Boise this morning, or…do we wait and go as scheduled two days from now. All those in favor of leaving in approximately two hours, raise your hand."

I waited to see what the group in general was thinking and how each of them were voting, especially Teddy. My vote was attached to Teddy's; When he raised his hand, so would I. Cautiously, I put my hand halfway up ready to extend fully the moment Teddy lifted his good arm or hand. He kept it down, as did Tina, Craig, and Matz, the same with Ritchie, Jenny, Barbie, Mindy, Matz's mother, and so on. Everyone's hand was down except for that of Shelley and her best friend Tracey.

"All those in favor of leaving at our scheduled time in two days, raise their hands." Again, I waited until Teddy raised his hand, making mine the last to go up.

My Bad Tequila

Shelley walked up to Teddy and blurted, "I thought you cared about your two friends, but noooo, you'd rather party for two more days."

Before Teddy could say a word I found myself by his side. "That is completely uncalled for. We all know Theodore is very upset, as we all are and should be."

Before I could finish, or before Shelley could muster a sinister jab at me, Teddy interrupted and said in an incredibly calm voice, "I think it will be better if we wait and see if we hear anything. Shelley, you heard the lady at the hotel say none of them have been seen at the hospital, which probably means they are lost or had car problems. If you want to take a bus into Hermosillo to look for them, I'll go with you. I really don't want to leave this country without my friends."

Shelley, now much calmer and more relaxed, replied, "Theodore, thank you! I'll think that over for a minute or two if you don't mind."

She tugged at Tracey's arm to leave the congregation and they walked towards the sea overlook.

I believe everyone was in awe of how well Teddy had handled the situation and "the difficult girl." In my head that was her label; it was a bit more generous than "Biatch," which could also easily have been her new alias.

Most everyone was now starting to disperse, as do ants after having their little work meeting underneath the earth. One by one, two by two, they make their way out into the world looking for something sweet. I, the lone worker ant, immediately found my own something sweet and was now standing next to Tina. Like the ant, I wanted to take the sweet thing I had found home. But the difference between the ant and me is that I would not want to share my newfound treat with the other ants.

My hand found Tina's and held it tight for a couple of seconds before saying anything to her. I turned to face Tina and before I could say anything, she put the words I was thinking back into the atmosphere. "I love you," she gently whispered, while looking into my astonished eyes.

How could something this beautiful and caring love me the way that I adored her? I whispered back, "Me too," and blew a quick, soft kiss for her to catch.

CHAPTER 9

The Fishing Trip
(El Viaje de Pescar)

Handing the captain over $35 of my Vegas-earned blackjack money, I turned to Tina and boomed, "Let's catch a big one, I want a trophy to remember this day."

Tina and I were on the boat without Teddy, who had selected to stay on land and wait for his friends after Shelley had made the decision to not take the bus into Hermosillo.

Just Tina and me, along with *Capitan Tiburon* (Captain Shark) and his first mate Jorge on the *Pez Vela* (Sailfish). This boat was part of the Catch-22 charter fleet, which was made up of four magnificent boats ranging from a 32-foot Luhrs convertible with twin Volvo diesel engines to a 25-foot Grady White. We were aboard a new 26-foot Grady White.

I knew this boat inside and outside, even though I had never been on one in the water. My experience with seeing a Grady White had been in Portland, Oregon at a boat show while attending an FFA (Future Farmers of America) function representing the Chapter of Marsing High School.

I had tried desperately to get at least one of my fellow FFA classmates to attend with me. We would need to leave the rodeo where I had just met the world-famous rodeo champion Larry Mahan at the indoor arena and ride the city bus a few miles to the huge international boat show.

The Great Mr. Larry Mahan signed my first semester's high school report card, which was the only thing I could find in my large leather billfold, which had been hand-stitched and stamped with a bull elk by yours truly in shop class. There were no other papers worthy of my rodeo hero's signature, so I thrust in front of him the report card which showed in detail that I had earned six As and one A minus. Mr. Mahan looked at the report card, caught a bit off guard, and then said, "Son, that's a mighty fine report card you got there," and started to hand it back to me.

"No, no," I pleaded while pushing it back. "Please sign it for me." "Well, young man, that would be a darn pleasure for me," he replied and signed my report card.

Here is what a person needs to know about the Great Mr. Larry Mahan. He was born November 21, 1943, in Salem, Oregon and became one of the first rodeo celebrities. He started competing as a professional in 1964, riding broncs and bulls. Two short years later, in 1966, he won his first all-around cowboy championship and held the title through 1970. In 1973, he won a record-setting sixth title. As a trendsetter, he helped promote professional rodeo and with his help the National Rodeo Association gained national exposure which brought in a much larger audience and fan base. He owned and flew his private plane, wore non-traditional loud plaid shirts, and wore his hair longer than the normal cowboy. He appealed to the media and appeared on several TV talk shows and in magazine ads. This cowboy retired from the professional rodeo circuit in 1977, incredibly having

My Bad Tequila

avoided any major injuries while appearing in over 1200 professional rodeos that spanned 18 years. The man is a living cowboy legend and a stud.

The reason I was carrying my prior semester's school grades around with me was that I knew how rare a feat I had accomplished. There had been only one other time I had come close to mastering this educational accomplishment and it had been much earlier in my already long nine-year school career.

In the third grade I earned all As, except for one B in science the first part of the semester. Wanting to get all As for the second half of the year, I studied science so hard that arithmetic missed my full attention and had failed me (or so it seemed at the time). Again I had all As and one lone B, but this time in math.

Anyhow, I got my autograph from the six-time All-Around Cowboy and went alone to the boat show in Portland. There I fell in love with the Grady White 25' Sailfish Boat with twin engines and a fiberglass hull. Never had I seen yachts and sea vessels of this magnitude. The boat was equipped with a cabin that included ba V-berth, a quarter berth on port side, and an enclosed head (toilet). The galley had a two-burner stove, an ice box, and a sink with storage underneath. As stated earlier, I knew the boat inside and out, because I had the full-color sales brochure sent to me just months earlier. When attending that boat show in 1974, I had signed up to receive sales information on the Grady White Boat Line. I had filled in the information and given it to one of the salesmen, telling him I was instructed to do so by my make-believe dad, and, poof, for the next decade I received colorful brochures of boats I would never be able to afford.

I explained in detail to Tina the nine-and-a-half-foot beam of the boat, its displacement weight of 5300 pounds, and its twin engines. I was excited and wanted Tina to share in the excitement. We were going deep sea fishing on a boat I had dreamed about for 13 years, a boat that I knew so well that the *capitan* thought my family owned one.

Our spectacular fishing vessel left the harbor at about noon. I had paid for a half day of fishing for Tina and me. The day before I had talked with the owner of the boat and told him that there would be three people fishing and he had quoted a price of $50.00 for a half day of deep-sea angling. Barnacle Bob had seen my immediate retreat reaction and had lowered the price to $40.00 including all beverages and lunch for the three of us. A handshake had occurred, and the expedition awaited.

However, when we arrived as only two people, a quick negotiation had occurred and $35.00 had been the determined outcome of that give and take. Had the truth been known to Bob the boat owner, I would have gladly paid twice that in cash (since I had over $100.00 in my pocket) to ride the open seas on this sacred Grady White Sailfish 25' boat with all the features a master boater could possibly want and or need.

We putted and jutted out of the harbor at five miles per hour so as to not create a wake that would disturb the other boats. The sun was high in the Mexico sky and albatross and pelicans flew above, behind, ahead of, and beside us. They seemed to be like a close family bidding us farewell as we made our way around the mountains that protected the marina and out to the open sea.

Once out of the protective bay area, our *capitan* pushed the throttle forward and our small yacht headed into chartered waters. I was on cloud nine though there were no clouds to be seen. The air was cool on our face, due to the breeze of our now-speeding boat, and occasionally water would slap up and cause a heavy mist of seawater to spray on our faces, arms and clothing. It felt fantastic, it smelled fantastic, it was fantastic. We were going to catch large fish, perhaps fish larger than Tina and me. Wow!!

For the time being we forgot about the troubles of our *amigos*, the missing threesome, and the schoolwork and studies that were awaiting our return to the University. At this moment all that mattered was the life of the sea and the sea of life.

I put my arm around Tina, who looked as radiant as I felt. For

My Bad Tequila

the first time in my life I felt my heart might explode because of how warm and large it felt. I loved each thing I set my eyes upon, each thing I had ever known, each person I had ever met. I thought to myself, "How could you have had wished you were dead all those times when you were growing up? Can't you now see it was all a foundation, building up to this great day?" I was overwhelmed with happiness. My light, salty tears were mixing with the heavy salt water from the Sea of Cortez, causing quite an exhilarating storm on my smiling face.

The boat slowed, bringing me back from my sightless cloud to a fiberglass structure on the sea. Jorge had rigged the poles with bright rubber-squid-looking lures that were about eight to ten inches long with large, fiercely sharp hooks hid towards the middle. After making sure the lures were attached correctly, he cast lightly underhand, sending the line into the seeming endless entity of water and letting the boat's forward movement put distance between us and the innocent-looking barbed hook.

As soon as Jorge had set as much line as he deemed necessary out to the sea, I climbed into the fishing chair. It was the first time I had ever sat in one, although it did resemble a barber's chair I had seen in my small hometown, of Marsing, Idaho. It looked a lot like Ike the Butcher's chair except it was white, unlike Ike's black chair. Ike the Butcher was the local barber. I don't know if he knew people substituted butcher for barber in his name. He was a pleasant man, bald with a single strand of hair, so no self-evidence of how great or not great he might be with hair clippers. I only visited him once on official business, when one of my younger brothers tried to cut my hair and did an awful job. When my mother returned home, she gave me $2.00 and sent me to Ike the Butcher. I was scared as I climbed into his chair and watched him mess with all his cutting utensils, sharpen his razor blade, and plug the clippers into the wall where I heard that horrible buzzing sound. At the end of about twenty minutes, Ike had told me I was free to leave. He did clean my head up quite well and balanced my hair out over my scalp. In fact, it didn't look bad at all.

But this chair, this chair was different. I wanted to sit in it for much longer than 20 minutes and while my heart throbbed as it did that day in Idaho, it was for different reasons.

The chair felt great, it swiveled from side to side and had a pole holder set right at the front center edge. This was living the dream. Now all I needed was the right fish to be swimming in the right place at the right time. Ten minutes quickly passed, my eyes straining to focus on the line for any change whatsoever. Then it hit. The line started screeching and I tensed up, ready for action. I waited for Jorge to grab the rod and set the hook good. He then put the pole in the holder for me and I began reeling frantically and maniacally until Jorge told me to slow down. Pull up and reel down, pull up and reel down. This action was much easier, and I kept with the pace, but it seemed as if tens of minutes had passed when actually it was about six minutes. This fish had to be large, was it a marlin or was it a sailfish? Jorge let out a yell that he saw it and grabbed the net.

"Why was he grabbing the net?" I wondered, "especially that small net?" My question was answered as a yellowfin tuna weighing about 35 pounds was brought on board. I was pleased, but a little disappointed.

"Berry good to eat, dees yellowtail," Jorge said while freeing the lure from the tuna's gills. "Nice size tuna, no?" he questioned or was that a statement?

"Yes," I replied, "very nice," and then added, "*Gracias*, Jorge."

Tina let out a gleeful yell and high-fived me. She was thoroughly enjoying this.

"You're up next *amiga*." I pointed to the chair as I went to her and planted a small peck on her cheek.

"You bet I am, and I'm going to catch a bigger one than that little guy," she said confidently.

Jorge, on cue, put the line back into the water and about five minutes later another screaming reel and Tina was hollering, "I've got one, I've got one."

The first mate again set the hook and placed the rod between Tina's legs. I shook my head as I didn't like the way that materialized

My Bad Tequila

in my mind. Tina began reeling, just as Jorge had instructed me to do, except Tina was doing it perfectly and I swear with a lot less jerk action than my movements had involved. She did complain that her arms were getting tired and that she wanted me to help her.

"No way, that's your fish, you're bringing it in all by your lonesome. I remember your remarks about my little fish," I reminded her, trying to stir some adrenaline into her weakening body.

Tina looked my way and then began focusing on the task at hand, bringing her monster fish into the boat. After a few more complaints and my returned barbs, she brought her fish to the back of the boat, where Jorge netted and secured her catch. Another yellowfin and, I'll be darned, it was slightly larger than mine. It was easy to tell when Jorge opened the large five-foot cooler tank to have Tina's fish join mine. Yep, it was longer and had more girth, probably 40 pounds or so. After the fish was secure and the boat was back to normal, I asked Jorge if we would catch any marlin or sailfish with the lure. "Maybeee," had been his response. Unsatisfied, I asked if we would have a better chance using something else such as live bait.

"*Si* (Yes), but you no want to catch yellowtail, berry good to eat," he answered, somewhat confused.

"*Si*, but I would rather catch a marlin, can we try?" I pleaded in my best fisherman tone.

"*No problemo*," came his response as he expertly undid the lure and tossed it down into the cabin, where it landed on the bed. He then lifted the cover off a square box tank holding water and several minnows about five to seven inches long. He grabbed a small net that looked as if it were for a household aquarium and scooped up two minnows. Grabbing the most active of the two he quickly slid the barbed hook into the center of the tiny fish and into the main part of its body so that it wiggled tremendously but was hooked and secure. Bait was ready, as all fish seem to be cannibalistic towards smaller fish. He gently tossed the bait into the sea and again let out line, set the drag, and then repeated the process with the other rod after reeling in the line and the lure we no longer needed to use.

I anxiously sat in the captain's chair for about 20 minutes, eyes again focused completely on rod, reel, and line. Soon I began to bore, climbed out of the chair and sat down beside Tina and waved Jorge over as my Scrabble-word mind was working on repeating Jorge's name in my head. "Hor hay" as it was pronounced was "Hey, Whore" in reverse. I shared the word game with Jorge, and he thought it was great, as his grasp of the English language was much more than he originally would have us to believe. To this day when I hear or see the name Jorge, I automatically think "Hey, Whore" and now you will as well, from this day forward.

I then remembered a story about fishing and began to narrate the story to Tina. Not completely a fishing story, really, it was more about partying, water skiing and hanging out with about 10 close friends. The only part about fishing is that one of my buddies had found a dead perch near the shoreline in Lake Cascade and had scooped it up to show us all. We had just come back from boating all day and were full of cheap beer—Pabst Blue Ribbon or Keystone, I think. I was pretty lit and grabbed the fish from my pal Roy and bit the head off. Why I did this, no idea, but all other nine guys in our weekend expedition loved it.

The governor of Idaho at the time, Cecil Andrus, was also returning with his family and friends after an enjoyable day on the water and caught my antics. He was disturbed by this action as we were staying at a cabin next to his. My friend Toby's parents owned a beautiful, two-story home in the woods and shared a dock with the governor and his family. I had never met the esteemed Governor Andrus; however, I had seen him on TV several times and recognized him immediately. Of course, I didn't realize it was him until it was too late, and I had a raw fish head in my mouth and the fish's body in my hand. Embarrassed and suddenly sober, I let the fish drop and spit the head out into the lake.

Toby bashfully said, "Hello Mr. and Mrs. Andrus," then added out of obligatory politeness, "These are my friends. We are staying up here for the Fourth of July weekend." Governor Andrus, his wife, his daughter, and three friends waved to us and said hello. Andrus then added, "We saw you and your friends out water skiing today."

Oh, shit! That was my only meeting with Cecil Andrus. A few minutes later, back inside the protective confines of the logs perfectly set together, we had a great laugh. Even Toby had to grin. He just hoped his political neighbors would not say anything to his politically correct parents about his asshole, dead-fish-biting friend who had also water skied nude around the lake twice that day, waving and screaming like a wild banshee at the previously peaceful boaters and anglers. Tina stopped me. "Tell me you didn't ski naked in front of the Idaho governor, wife, and daughter and tell me you didn't actually bite the head off a dead fish."

"Okay, I won't tell you." Then I continued. "I didn't know it was them or that they were out there. I do wish that it wouldn't have happened but hey, we all had a great time that weekend. Besides, the fish was dead, it wasn't like I did an Alice Cooper or Ozzy Osbourne, biting off the head of a live bat or chicken and drinking its blood."

"Alice Cooper didn't bite off a fowl's head, nor did he drink the blood of a chicken," said Tina, defending one of her favorite rockers. "He thought the chicken could fly and tossed it up, thinking it would soar away, but it came down on the crowd; it was the concert goers that tore the chicken to shreds, not Alice," she continued, still trying to salvage Alice Cooper's reputation.

Jorge brought me back to the present as he picked up one of the poles and began to reel it in fairly rapidly. So happened, he was checking the live bait, which was now dead and lifeless. Taking it off the hook, he threw it into the large body of endless water, scooped another minnow, and again we had a squirmer on the end of our line. He continued doing this about every 15 to 20 minutes and each time the minnow had either lost the will to live, been drowned by being whipped through the water at our trolling pace or had been so internally injured that death had taken place.

I continued with my story, telling Tina of our going into McCall, Idaho the next day for the Fourth of July celebration and fireworks on the lake. In the middle of telling her about the town of McCall, how it had the nickname "Ski Town USA" because it was surrounded by the cold, clear Payette Lake where water skiing in the summer was a chosen pastime and a nearby ski resort took advantage of the heavy snowfall in the winter for snow skiers. McCall was my favorite place in all of Idaho, my favorite place in all of the world as I knew it, from my humble existence as a non-traveler or adventurer outside the state. This resort town was located approximately 120 miles north of Boise, about a three-hour drive along the Payette River and about 30 minutes from Cascade Lake, the manmade reservoir lake where we were staying.

"The 10 of us arrived at McCall later than what we had planned on, at about 4:00 p.m. We decided to go to a bar on the lake called 'The Yacht Club,' which had a large balcony overlooking Payette Lake, with its million-dollar vacation homes and gigantic ponderosas. Arriving late, we each paid our own cover charge into the over-crowded landmark, pushing, shoving and excusing ourselves until reaching the bar. Through the plate-glass windows we could see the lake, as well as the partygoers huddled and packed on the redwood deck. A couple of us made our way to the door that led to the open air but we were quickly turned away by three overweight and above-medium-height bouncers. We were told that nobody else was getting out on the deck, only those who had arrived early and secured the premium firework-watching spaces.

"Reluctantly we joined the other eight near the packed bar. I was pissed and could think of nothing else but getting out on that deck.

"I guzzled my Coors Light and had downed nearly another when the answer to our predicament came to me. I quickly told the guys that I had an idea of how to get us all outside. I turned to my buddy Richard and said, 'You need to be my yes man.' Richard knew how to behave, how to act, and how to go along with anything I tried. We had been friends for about three years and most of the time we had spent together had been in a bar, at a party, or in one of our apartments. Our time together always had one thing in common—drinking.

My Bad Tequila

Drinking by itself or for just the sake of drinking is boring; however, if you habitually add a fun component on how to accomplish a special feat or do something interesting then drinking can be quite educational and fun. Together we had come up with some fantastic stories that had gotten us laid, into concerts, or upgraded at sporting events. We knew how to manipulate whoever was in charge by embellishment, by changing the story just a bit, or by flat ass telling a whopper. It was all about making the story completely and unequivocally believable.

"Finishing my last swig of beer followed by a quick shot of well tequila, I popped a Tic Tac into my mouth and asked the bartender if the manager or owner was around. The girl behind the bar pointed to the opposite end of the bar, where a middle-aged man with a handlebar mustache was filling mugs of beer. Richard and I inched our way through the masses of college kids, locals, and summer forest firefighters. 'Excuse me sir,' I-all but-yelled at the proprietor of the fine establishment. 'Are you the owner of this place?' I questioned, knowing full well that he was the person I needed to speak with. 'Yes, I am,' he replied.

"'Well, I need to talk to you about something very serious,' I warned.

"'I'm very busy right now, we can talk later?'

"'What I need to talk with you about is extremely important,' I said, and to add emphasis, I continued, 'It could be a matter of life or death.' His attention now was fully on me, and he led us towards the bathrooms. Richard and I followed him towards the entrance of where we had entered. Here, there were not as many bodies, and it was much quieter. I introduced Richard and myself as Richard Scott and Rhet Richards of Richard and Richards Architectural Firm from Boise. He said his name was Jim, and we all shook hands. I led the way to the door and we walked down the steps, out onto the cracked sidewalk, and onto the grass that sloped towards the lake and surrounded the building. From here we could see the deck above and the beams holding the deck from below. I told Jim that Richard and I were heavily schooled in the field of engineering and architectural design and that having seen so many individuals on his deck I had become concerned about the excess weight and stress being put upon the beams and foundation. I proceeded to point out knots and cuts in the large beams, which made him extremely nervous. He asked me, 'Do you think it's unsafe?'

"With a grim, stern face I looked him in the eye and said, 'I would not make up something this serious or kid you on our nation's birthday. If you don't get those people off your deck, there could be injuries, lawsuits and perhaps fatalities.'

"'Oh my gosh, what should I do?' He asked, shaking and now in a panic mode.

"'Listen, I am here with nine friends, we'll help your bouncers get everyone off the deck,'" I offered.

It was at this time Tina interrupted my story. "Oh my goodness! Now I know where I've seen you before. It was YOU on that deck, you were one of the guys who made my friends and I leave our great seats on that deck. You little lying bastard." Tina gave me a slight shove and then began to laugh.

"Well, should I continue?" I asked as I, too, chuckled at the coincidence. This made the story even more of a classic.

"Remember, I told you from the beginning that I recognized you and sure enough, that was it." Tina was happy that the puzzle in her mind had been solved. No more wondering or trying to figure out how she knew me. I had always figured she had mistaken me with someone who could have looked similar; but no, she had been correct all along.

"Go ahead and finish," she said, and again she smiled and shook her head.

"Well, we got everyone cleared off the deck, as you know. and then the owner asked me how he could ever repay me. 'Why not let me and my buddies hang out on the deck, watch the fireworks and give us a discount on our drinks for the rest of the evening,' I suggested.

"Jim did even better than that. All night our drinks were on the house, and he had five pizzas and four dozen wings delivered out

My Bad Tequila

to that structurally-sound deck. What an incredible night of fireworks off the lake, with you and everyone else peering out the windows."

Jorge then caught my attention. "*Senor* Rhet, deese is our last feeesh for bait."

Shit, our last chance at getting a marlin and the wind was blowing harder; nasty, dark clouds were forming, and the temperature was dropping. I saw Tina shudder from the brisk breeze and the occasional seawater spray that was finding our bare skin to plant its moisture. I watched intently as Jorge, a fishing craftsman, put the last minnow perfectly onto a hook, cast gently into the not-so-gentle waters, and let the line dissolve into the endless laps of waves.

The boat was rocking furiously, and we held onto any part of the vessel that we could find would allow us to be somewhat steadfast and secure. Tina called out to Jorge, "Do you have any life jackets?" Jorge lifted a bench and showed her eight new life vests still in their clear packaging. "*Si*, but we never had to use," he said, not wanting to break the streak of still having unworn vests.

"We'll both take a vest," I demanded as I cautiously made my way over to Jorge and the bright orange vests. I grabbed two and tossed one to Tina, not checking to see if there were size variations.

I noticed Jorge wince as we tore the light plastic film that separated a new vest from the now used vest. I could tell he was doing a mental count in his head, "now there eess six new vests and two that people can wear." We put them on and the storm seemed to subside. It was at this moment the *capitan* yelled "marlin" and pointed. I had never seen this sight. AIt was the top fin of the marlin glistening as a ray of sun had found its way in front of a cloud.

The *capitan* turned the boat and Jorge quickly gathered in the line. As we headed towards the single fin swimming in the sea, and neared the boat to the large fish, Jorge cast our last piece of bait 20 yards and perfectly in front of the swimming marlin's direction. He had just set the drag when the line started screaming and Jorge yanked back on the pole, setting the hook. In a flash I was in the fishing chair and Jorge was struggling to get the rod into its safety hole at the front of the chair between my legs. The *capitan* had slowed the boat to nearly a crawl.

I, too, grabbed the pole that looked as if it wanted to follow the marlin into the open sea instead of bringing the marlin to us. Together we managed to place the rod in the swivel holder, and I took over. I pulled back and reeled down. The marlin took a magnificent leap straight up into the air and it was a gorgeous sight to see such a mammoth sea creature. Taking full advantage of the slack in the line, I reeled and reeled furiously, like a hungry mad man who did not want to lose his fish or meal. My adrenaline was full speed and instant energy had come fully into my body.

The constant pulling up and reeling in was tiring, but I continued. Never in my life had I wanted a fish so badly. This was one fish I did not and was not going to lose. Again, the beautiful creature left the water and looked as if it was dancing on its back fin, standing erect, its sword reaching for the heavens. "How large is it?" I yelled to Jorge.

Tina responded first. "It's huge, it's huge," she shouted with arms spread as wide as her extended reach would allow.

"*Si, si*, it is a beeg one, maybe one hundred fifty pounds, maybe more," Jorge chimed in, agreeing with Tina.

I continued the reeling sequence I had memorized years earlier in my dreams; but I was beginning to weaken now that 15 minutes had gone by, and a bit of the adrenaline had passed. Calling out to Tina, I asked if she could peel me an orange. I needed some energy, and quick.

Before I knew it she was putting tiny oranges slices to my lips and I was being revitalized via healthy fruit. Arms now feeling strong again, I once again started making headway with the marlin. I imagined it was getting near the boat, but it hadn't shown itself.

Jorge told me to stop reeling and I distressedly screamed, "What happened to my fish?"

"It is heere, neeer theee boat," he said calmly, while he grabbed up his gaffe.

As Jorge leaned over the boat to look for the fish, the giant marlin leapt into the air and looked at us all in the boat, especially Jorge with the gaffe. The monstrous fish thrust itself at the boat, and at Jorge. The marlin had known that death and his captors were near and had chosen to fight until its death, which meant leaving the safety of his turf, the sea, to fight in a world he knew nothing about, a world where he couldn't survive.

Jorge saw what the fish was determined to do, and tried to move aside, but not quickly enough. The sharp end of the marlin's sword caught Jorge on the right side of his stomach, tearing his shirt and puncturing the skin. Jorge screamed in agony, "*El pinche marlin apunalar a me.*" English translation: "The fucking marlin stabbed me."

The marlin was on our boat and madly thrashing about, its big eyes looking at us each time it tried to jump. Tina and I were on the opposite side of the boat as I had made my way out of the fishing chair upon seeing the giant fish coming at Jorge in midair. The captain had shut off the noisy boat and the sounds of Jorge in pain and the fish in pain were deafening. The captain had found a small bat and began beating the marlin in the head, strong blow after strong blow as if each one was saying, "this is for Jorge, and this is for Jorge, you mean, ornery, fucking fish."

Jorge had grabbed the first aid kit and gone down below deck and Tina had followed.

"How bad is it?" I hollered down to Tina.

"Pretty bad wound," she bellowed back to me, then added, "it looks awfully deep."

"What fucking else can go wrong on this trip?" I thought, not having the enjoyment of the catch I had pictured in my mind for so long. The *capitan* had quit beating the fish to the head. He was finally convinced it was fully dead and had received its earned death sentence for injuring his first mate. The "Skipper" then went down the stairs to check on his "Little Buddy."

I walked over and stood above my prize fish, his color now a dull, grayish brown. The vibrant, beautiful blue had left its body at about the same time life had left it. How strange I pondered. "Blue and

Life" and "Gray and Death" but, "we're blue when there is death and everything seems gray."

Maybe there is a connection between life and death.

Only one of my *amigos* came back out into the open air. The wind had calmed, most of the clouds had passed, and blue skies were again showing themselves. "How's Jorge?" were the first words from my mouth as Tina reappeared.

"Doing pretty good. You can go down and see him if you want," came her reassuring words. Jorge was shirtless, and lying on his back, eyes open and alert. A large, blood-drenched bandage about six inches by six inches was taped to his side. Thank goodness it was much farther to the right than I had first believed it to be. Tina was able to get most of the bleeding to stop and with Jorge lying still and the wound facing upward, there was a great chance it would not bleed heavily again.

The captain had not bothered to take the time to clean the fish blood from the boat. He turned the switch to on, the loud diesel motor sounded, and we were on our way back to the marina.

"Man, that is quite a fish you caught there, Mr. Rhet, the fisherman," Tina said playfully.

"Yeah; but, geez, I wish it hadn't gone after Jorge," I replied.

"He is going to be okay; a few stitches will be needed and some rest," Tina consoled me by saying, then added, "It wasn't your fault, he'll be alright."

I smiled and kissed her on the cheek while reaching for her camera. I took pictures of my prizes: first of my Tina and then of my marlin.

I had caught both the girl and the fish of my dreams.

The *ambulancia*, the taxidermist contact, the cameraman, the scaling guy, and the fish meat butcher, along with some of their families, were all awaiting our return. The marina was abuzz as the *capitan* had radioed ahead that we had an injured first mate who needed to be sewn up and a large marlin that needed to be weighed, photographed with the proud fisherman, mounted for future display, cleaned and eaten.

Everyone wanted and everyone was going to get a piece of the action.

Jorge walked off the boat and as he neared the end of the dock, I remembered I had not tipped him. I called out to him, and he turned and waited for me. I handed him a ten-dollar bill, said *gracias* to him and extended my hand. That ten dollars was well worth the huge smile and handshake he gave me with his left hand. He didn't want to raise or move his right arm and hand any more than necessary. He then climbed into the same *ambulancia* that Teddy had been hauled off in a couple of days earlier. I was starting to think the term "meat wagon" is a very fitting word for ambulance.

After the *amublancia* screamed away with its siren blaring, the marina was alive with laughter and shouting as everyone knew a small payday was about to be had. I went through most of my blackjack money, tipping the *capitan*, the fish-weighing guy, the taxidermist contact guy, and the professional photographer for the lasting memory.

I did not have to tip the families that were going to clean and eat the 180-pound fish. The marlin was five pounds heavier than its angler and a lot tastier. We did keep a few tuna steak cuts and had them wrapped in baggies for the lovely fish dinner we had planned for our last night. Nothing much better than fresh tuna on the grill and the bragging rights of having brought in a fighting marlin.

Walking back from the marina with a huge smile planted on my face, I strolled back to the hotel with Tina's hand in mine, hoping to see the Suburban parked near the bus.

Rico & Connie in
Cabo San Lucas, Mexico

Rico deep sea fishing with
Amigos in Mazatlan, Mexico

Pictured left to right:
Louie, Rico, Greg,
Howie, Rick, Richard

My Bad Tequila

CHAPTER 10

Tina and Our Lives
(Tina y Nuestra Vidas)

No Suburban. Our hearts and hopes collapsed at the same time. There was no one to be seen in the parking lot, just the lonely school bus we had ridden on this journey.

I smelled of fish but was in no hurry to rid myself of this odor as it reminded me of my catch and of the glorious afternoon on the water. I suggested to Tina I would quickly wash up, (meaning my hands would have cool water run over them with no soap and a quick splash of water would find its way upon my face). I wanted to keep that fishy smell, that fisherman's smell, on me. We both needed to use the *baño*, so decided to meet out front in *cinco minutos* (five minutes), but not in "Mexican minutes."

Opening the door to my room, I strongly hoped Teddy would not be in there for unselfish reasons. Quickly I scanned the tiny room and saw to my great satisfaction there was no Teddy. "Great," I thought to myself, "he is out and about, hopefully enjoying this small resort town, and the food or the drink that this country offered."

Back outside I sniffed my hands to see if I could still smell the hint of the sea and of fish on my hands. Smiling to myself slightly, the aroma was still there. Not quite as strong, but it was there. I had not seen Tina leave her room, but she had seen me smelling my hands and made sure to comment on it.

"What in the hell were you doing?" she questioned me, hoping to arouse some sort of light embarrassment in me.

"Well, I wasn't picking my nose, if that's what you mean. I was just seeing if I still smelled of fish, and to my pleasure, I sure do."

"You are truly weird, you do know that don't you?" she teased. "Yep, and that is why you love me, right!" I had blurted this before clearly thinking about what I had just said.

"*Absolutamente* (Absolutely)," came her reply as she took my hand in hers.

"I touched the sky, it felt like air! Only more real," were my serene thoughts.

We decided on a quick bite to eat at La Palapa, a small open restaurant on the beach owned and operated by a Greek man. Then a walk on the beach would finish off the day perfectly. Tina ordered a beef taco and bottled water, I had the *numero tres* (number three), which consisted of a Gyro and a Pacifico beer.

The sand on the beach south of town was incredibly soft and felt of flour. Our beach walk was on the strand called *San Francisco Playa*, or San Francisco Beach for the gringos. Once we were on the outskirts of town the beach was fairly uninhabited except for the occasional small condo complex or a restaurant such as the Fiesta parked on the edge of the shoreline.

Our conversation that late afternoon and early evening was dominated by our childhoods, our lives, our parents, our dislikes and our likes.

Tina had grown up in eastern Washington as a wealthy fruit

My Bad Tequila

grower's daughter near Yakima. Her dad, like his dad, had worked on the fruit ranch for his father and had inherited the business. Tina was fourth generation of the Valentino clan; her great-grandfather had landed at New York's Ellis Island from Italy when he was 14 years of age with an older brother who was 16. The two young Valentinos had come to the United States of America to make their new start and way on life. After living in New York for two years upon arrival from Europe, they decided to make way for the West. St. Louis had been their destination of choice, but having spent a month and half in Missouri they became restless as murmurings of a new land even farther west were beginning to spread.

The Valentino duo made their way to the Columbia River and chose to settle in the Yakima Valley just a hundred miles from there as water was plentiful, the land was fairly flat, and the winters were mild. Each brother claimed 660 acres side by side, which gave them a combined two square miles of the best farmland in all the eastern Washington basin. They had immediately begun purchasing horses and plows from neighboring farms and started plowing and tilling the rich earth. Within the first two years each had taken young brides, both sisters of a nearby farmer who had also been a settling immigrant to the new land from Sweden. Their father-in-law eventually passed away with no sons and the four sisters inherited the farm, making it possible for the Valentino brothers and their wives to buy out the other two sisters and turn another 660 acres into orchards and vineyards.

Over the years, the Valentino family had acquired more and more acreage and Tina's family now had more than five square miles of the most fertile land in the state of Washington. Her father had become involved in local politics and was now one of two U.S. Senators for Washington state. Tina had told me that her father was a hardworking and determined man, but also, she described him as cold and unloving. Her mother, though, was extremely caring and warm. She awakened Tina each morning with a kiss on the cheek and her favorite wake-up phrase: "It's time to get up, Honey, and greet the new day!"

While Tina was telling me this, I thought about how there were similar points in our lives, yet how much different our lives were and had evolved. My dad, when home, had worked for a wealthy fruit farmer, who had become a Gem State (Idaho) Congressman. All five of us boys at one time or another had worked side-by-side with our dad on the Sunnyslope orchards in Idaho near the Snake River. We had picked cherries, apples, peaches, pears, plums, and apricots. We had pruned trees, mowed the grass, and picked the weeds that grew between the trees. We had changed sprinkler pipes so the trees would get enough water needed to grow healthy and bear fruit.

Instead of being awoken each morning with a kiss on the cheek or the lick of a puppy's tongue on her face as with Tina's childhood, my mother would come into the bedroom I shared with my siblings and say, "Rhet, it's time to get up and face the wicked, old world," then leave the room and begin heating water on the stove for our breakfast of hot oatmeal. Once in a great while when my mother was in a soft, good mood, she would awaken me with the words, "Rise and shine, looks like it might be a nice day out." Those times were few, but so pleasant.

I remember seeing a tender side of her on one occasion. It was on Christmas Eve of 1974, one of the years I didn't see my dad for several months due to his heavy drinking. That Idaho winter was one of the coldest on record to this date. It was a cold and snowy late afternoon, on December 24th; all five boys and our mother were wearing layers of clothing to keep warm in our 12 x 60-foot mobile home. Blankets were strewn on the couch, where we bundled together to stay warm on that holiday evening. No gifts, no heat, no candy canes were in the house, but we did have joy, laughter, love, cookies, and hot tea to help give us warmth (oh, and we had potatoes, lots of potatoes). My brothers and I sang Christmas carols and tried to console our mother by telling her we didn't need any presents as we had each other, a home, and a GOD that loved us.

Suddenly we fell quiet as an unexpected car pulled in front of our trailer house. The six of us peered out at a lady who stepped out of

My Bad Tequila

a four-door gray sedan, covered in red from head to foot with a hat, gloves, a heavy coat, and shiny boots. We watched intensely as she opened the trunk of her car and pulled out a large green canvas military-style bag. Immediately we started working on loosening up the partially frozen sliding-glass door to let our unknown guest into our home. With the canvas bag slung over her shoulder, she climbed the wooden steps to our humble abode and came inside.

Once our guest came into our home she asked, "Are you the Austen family?"

"Yes," "Yes," "Yes," "Yes," "Yes," came the replies from five curious boys, dying to see what was in the large green bag. The lady looked at my mother and said these words. "Well, I am with the Salvation Army, and we received information that your family could not afford gifts for Christmas, so I have brought gifts of toys and clothes donated for you." The angel of a woman had barely finished her introduction, when my mother replied, quite harshly, "We do not accept charity!" The Salvation Army woman began to explain further that it was not considered charity, but my mother continued her vehement stance,

"This family will not accept these gifts," she said. "Thank you for coming." The lady picked up the bag, again slung it over her shoulder, and headed back into the cold. Our mother turned and saw her five distressed young men who would have a hard time singing any more Christmas Carols that evening and she hung her head. She slid open the door and called out to the lady, as stoic as possible, "Please come back in. Each of my boys can choose one item a piece." She then looked at me, smiled, and said, "Go help the lady carry the bag."

Five young boys squealed with pleasure, the oldest at fourteen, the youngest at seven years of age, the other three in between. She was the "Christmas Angel" or "Santa's Helper," as she was honorably named many things that evening. She from the Salvation Army came into the house with a huge smile. Gently she opened the "Santa Claus Sack" and put all the contents onto the linoleum floor. We carefully analyzed each item as if they were diamonds, jades, pearls, gold, and sterling silver. I knew what gift was mine the instant I saw it leave the bag: a great-looking used McGregor leather baseball mitt. I put that leather-stitched ball glove on my left hand, and it fit perfectly. I do not remember what my four brothers chose, that beautiful Christmas Eve, but, I do remember all of them being as pleased and thankful with their gifts as was I with mine. I looked at my mother with more love than I had ever felt for her, knowing she had made the choice of bringing joy to her sons over her strong sense of pride. She had suffered humiliation as a human being but had triumphed as a mother of goodness.

My youngest sibling still believed in Santa Claus, so we concocted a story that the lady was a friend of St. Nicholas and was helping him out that night as he was so busy with other children's deliveries around the world. We would celebrate three more Christmas Eves and Days together as a family before the youngest was taken from us in this world to be an angel in heaven. He was lucky that he was still a believer in Santa Claus when his life had ended in a tragic accident. Little Steven broke his neck falling from our apricot tree while playing and enjoying life.

The next Christmas that rolled around after Steven's death never heard a Christmas tune in the Austen household; all of us were still grieving. We never got over not having our littlest brother asking questions about Santa Claus, his elves, his reindeer, and the North Pole. It took me tens of years to again enjoy the Christmas holiday, and it is still my least favorite time of year.

Looking back now at the way I was aroused from sleep as a youngster I realize it was just my mother's only way of toughening me up for what cold reality lay ahead for me and my younger brothers. Through most of my childhood I was considered the man of the house when my dad was not at home, either because he had left us again or because he was driving a semi-truck and trailer across the continental forty-eight states. When I was about 12 years old, I dreamed of going to heaven and sitting at a huge, gorgeous wooden table with gigantic wooden chairs and eating oatmeal. I believe the dream stemmed from my daily pondering how nice it must be in heaven as preached to me on Sunday sermons in the little white church we attended. At some level I wanted to leave the only world I knew and get on with the afterlife of no sorrow and no responsibility. Odd, though, that oatmeal was my meal of choice, it seemed, whether in heaven or on earth.

Tina had attended private Catholic schools where she had learned to read, write, and speak proper Spanish and Latin.

I had learned Spanglish by working in the orchards and fields alongside the Mexican immigrants. One man, named Ernesto, was a foreman of sorts as he was supplied with a 30-foot rusted trailer with a termite-infested wood interior and partly covered vinyl floors where it had not completely rotted. The trailer had been placed completely out of sight of all the packing sheds and other small homes where some workers stayed and paid rent to the wealthy ranch owner. Ernesto had lived in that same trailer for 11 years before my brothers and I met him. The old Mexican man was approximately 50 years of age, ancient by our young standards. He was an excellent worker and would occasionally help us change the sprinklers in the summertime. He would invite my two younger brothers and me over to his trailer for a *cerveza* and we would struggle to understand his stories with his broken English and strong accent. He would let us all share one beer as he told us we were deserving as men, because we had worked as hard as any man he had worked alongside. We had told our mother of Ernesto and his friendship but never of the beer, as we had a strong feeling she would be extremely upset and possibly upset the apple cart, figuratively and physically.

As I thought about Ernesto a sadness engulfed me as I recalled the day I heard of his death. U.S. border agents had received an anonymous tip about some illegal aliens hiding and living in the fruit orchards and had come north to investigate. Ernesto had been discovered. Scared, he ran from the pursuing agents and was gunned down with no less than seven shots to his back as he tried to escape and maintain freedom. My mother had told me the news about five years earlier and I had silently grieved for my old friend, with whom I had shared my first beer and a few more after that.

Tina had told me about the fun times of growing up in an orchard and of her horses and many other pets. She, like me, loved most academic subjects and school. But unlike me, she had never received a swat at school or had been in trouble. That is where the differences really began to make themselves visible. I had been in trouble several times, and been swatted by most of my principals, of whom had pet names for their paddles such as the "Green Hornet," a solid inch and a half of wood that was nearly three feet long, with a handle of approximately twelve inches for a great windup and six strategically drilled holes in the butt of the paddle for a sharper, more penetrating and aching effect. I had personally met the "Green Hornet" three times, one of which was at an all-high school and eighth grade assembly that had been called to maximize the embarrassment factor. Mr. Laymoth served as school principal and head basketball coach for the varsity team and was a stout man at six foot one inch tall and weighing 200 pounds with a marine-style crew cut. He announced to the student body that Rhet, a freshman, had agreed to take his swat in front of all Marsing classmates. This agreement had come minutes earlier when Laymoth and I had been discussing the frequency of my visits to his boring office with its pictures of his much-too-heavy wife and two children who looked as conceited and confused as their father. Mr. Laymoth had suggested something different needed to be done to perhaps change my attitude at school and the public beating was agreed upon.

  The strange assembly announcement drew a quickened hush to the usual noisy group of gathering students. I waved at the crowd, paying special attention to seeking out my friends on the bleachers. This brought a roar of laughter from the previously quiet crowd and pissed off Laymoth even more. I bent over sideways to give all students a good viewing and let the principal swing back and crack my ass. The noise was great, but not as great as the pain. I had no idea so many nerves were connected from the butt to the brain, and I wanted to immediately pass out from the agony. Instead, I straightened myself, grimaced one last time and again waved to the crowd. Laymoth never

My Bad Tequila

again called for an assembly to try and humiliate another student.

This incident and the next story were to become defining moments for the rest of my high school years of not being tormented by upper classmen.

I was the smallest boy in my class since about first grade. I would not start to catch up and outgrow some of my classmates until my junior year, the same year I graduated from high school at the age of 16.

My being the smallest of my peers made me an easy target for bullies; so had, my refusal to accept my role as the kid who gets put in the trash can or hung by his jock strap from the basketball rim. Kids with any perceived flaw make for even greater fun for the idiots who get off on mistreating other less developed humans. It didn't matter to these Neanderthals or to neighboring Neanderthals in other school districts if the flaw was physical, mental, or economical. The worst of the worst was a senior named Lennie Assaholman, who had messed with me all my eighth-grade year when he was a junior and now having received senior status was even more hellbent on treating the little freshman to blows to the crown of the head with his class ring turned to the inside palm. Another big hit for the Neanderthals, in these small rural Idaho towns during the spring when the canals would be filling up with water for crops and cattle, was to roundup freshman guys and heave them into the dirty, cow-and-horse-shit-infected canal water. This was a yearly ritual and I had been selected several times as an eighth grader and twice as a freshman by Lennie, Squiggy's a-hole friend. It was the second time that year that finally I reached my point of no return. Lennie had spotted me walking home from school with one of my brothers. He was driving his fancy bright yellow Ford truck with four-wheel drive and came roaring upon us. We began to run as we were on Canal Street, the same street where we lived, our trailer house semi-permanently parked just 10 feet from the road. Lennie caught my younger seventh-grade brother easily and tossed him into the flowing canal; I went back to try and help my brother out of the water when he pushed me in. It was on a Monday and our clothes were still clean as we tried to wear our jeans three days in a row because of the cost of washing, including water, detergent, and the work of hanging five boys' jeans on a clothesline. I was pissed and Lennie was laughing as he climbed into his monster yellow truck.

My younger brother and I walked home and changed, and I swore to each of my younger brothers that Lennie Assaholman would never again bother any of the five of us. Each of my siblings looked at me as if I were a crazed lunatic because Lennie could bother anyone he wanted; supposedly, he was the toughest *hombre* in Marsing, Idaho. But I didn't care, and I had a plan. Lennie had a crush on his best friend's younger sister, Deanna; she and her older brother lived just below us in a nice two-story ranch house with a covered carport, an extended driveway, and a basketball hoop set up for neighborhood pickup games. In the past, we would see Lennie's truck parked there on the smooth concrete driveway almost daily as the son of a bitch didn't have to work. I think he stole lunch money and some of the wealthier kids gladly paid him not to torment them. Fuming, with my hair still damp, I saw Lennie's bumblebee yellow Ford in the driveway of his buddy's home. I went to my room and got a ball of kite yarn and retrieved some matches I had found when I stumbled upon two of my brothers trying to smoke cigarettes behind the tiny shed adjacent to our trailer. I walked directly to Lennie's Ford truck, set on the pavement at the Eddger place where Lennie was a constant visitor, unscrewed the gas tank, put in the end of the yarn and began unwinding the string as I made my way back up to Canal Street and our home.

I then took the matches from my pocket, with my brothers all watching in disbelief at my schizophrenic mind and hands doing something we all knew would and could only end badly. They begged me to not light the first match; but I did so, and the string quickly extinguished. I reached for another, same results; another, this time the fire sizzled for a couple of feet before fizzling. This went on for almost the entire matchbook and I was very near the truck, about 20 feet away with my brothers still in tow begging me to stop. It was then that

My Bad Tequila

Lennie came running out of the house but stopped short of the stoop as he saw me in anticipation of striking another match. He didn't know I had already lit tens of matches and the chances of this being the fatal match strike was close to zero. He pleaded with me not to strike the fire. I saw my negotiating advantage and was beginning to think a bit clearly of the consequences of blowing up a vehicle and possibly innocent neighbors' homes and lives. I looked Lennie squarely in the eyes and said, "If ever you touch me or one of my brothers again, life as you know it will never be the same." He started weeping like a little schoolgirl right there in front of me, my brothers, and the young lady he had been trying to woo who had come outside to see what the crying and begging was about.

Lennie Assaholman agreed to never say or do anything to the Austen clan for as long as he had breath of life. But he did add that if anything happened to his precious truck, I would be the first person he would come searching for. My brothers looked at me in astonishment and admiration as I went over and pulled the string from the gas tank and screwed the cap on tight. If I had been a professional demolitionist or had thought out my plan longer, I'm sure I would have come to the conclusion that you have to soak the string in gasoline before venturing to ignite it. To this day, I think of what a disaster that day could have been. Instead, after that day nobody ever messed with an Austen again in Marsing. Even my friends were afraid to snap me with a towel in the locker room or shower after physical education class.

After sharing with Tina this part of my teen life, she came back with a family tale even more mind blowing. She finally opened about her "lost" brother.

Yes, Tina and I were a lot alike but, very different too. She was much saner, but I was the better Scrabble player. Or so I thought.

Top Picture – Author's Mom and Dad on Wedding Day with 51 Ford Hardtop, August 1959

Middle Picture – Baby Rico and Dad on first fishing trip in Payette, Idaho in Summer of 1960

Bottom Picture – 5 Austin Brothers, 1st day of School in front of trailer home, August 1973 Marsing, Idaho; back row: David & Rico; front row Steven, Samuel & Michael

My Bad Tequila

CHAPTER 11

The Ring
(El Anillo)

As we headed back to our group headquarters at the motel, an old Mexican woman balancing a stack of bright, colorful sombreros on her mighty head, woven Mexican blankets draped over her drooping shoulder, and carrying a gigantic briefcase stopped to show us her wares. Ten feet behind her, walking barefoot in the sand and wearing nothing but worn blue underpants and a dirty T-shirt, was a bow-legged toddler. The little boy had to be no older than thirty-six months of age and carried a small box filled with chiclets. The *señora* (woman) took the opportunity to rest as she delicately lifted the 10-plus sombreros from her head and laid them on one of the wool blankets she had removed from shoulder. The baby vendor dragged his little feet through the soft, thick sand and asked, "Chiclet, chiclet, *amigo?*" in his squeaky and childish Spanish accent which seemed more fitting for a cartoon character than a three-year-old *bambino* (baby). That little *chico* (boy) was a true salesman as he had me pulling *dinero* from my shorts before his brief pitch was over.

While I was choosing my flavor of chiclets and deciding how many *pesos* would be an acceptable price for a foot-and-a-half tall beach hawker, Tina had started to ooh and ahh, saying *bonita* (beautiful feminine) this and *bonito* (beautiful masculine) that, as she fumbled through the silver and turquoise jewelry the short Mexican mother had stored in her leather suitcase. I ended up exchanging with the child a crisp U.S. dollar bill and a ten-*peso* piece for two small packages of hard, ancient gum, one pink and the other green. The bartering baby jumped up and down and shouted, "*Gracias! Gracias!*" as he clearly knew the value of a dollar. He then held the dollar and the *peso* coin as high as his short, fat arms could reach, bellowing to this mother, "*Mama, mama, mira* (look), *mira, mama, mucho mama.*" His mother smiled, gently took the money from the child, and patted his black hair while soothingly saying, "*Bueno, bueno mi hijo pequeno* (good, my little son)," which put the proudest smile on the pint-sized *amigo*.

I joined Tina in looking at the necklaces, bracelets, rings, chokers, and earrings. My eye caught a glistening silver ring with two dolphins intertwined at their necks on the front of the ring and their tails touching on the smaller back of the ring. Picking it up, I examined it closely. Tina gasped when she saw it, and I slipped it on her left ring finger. It slid on with perfection, as though it had been made especially for her. Her lips trembled and she whispered to me it was the most beautiful ring she had ever placed upon her hand. Without hesitation, I asked the woman bearing gifts the price, and after a quick negotiation it was Tina's. She lifted my hand to her mouth and softly put her crimson lips on the back of my hand, thanking me over and over while whispering, "This will always be my most favorite lucky ring."

We said our *adioses* to the selling duo and held each other tightly as we walked to the parking lot.

We both stared unbelievingly at the Suburban parked at the edge of the lot. The vehicle was back, but not in the same condition as

My Bad Tequila

when it had left. Fire had destroyed the entire interior and carcass of the Suburban. No longer was there upholstery, tires, mirrors, or windows. It looked like it had been struck by a bomb in Vietnam—honestly looked better than most such vehicles I had witnessed seeing on the NBC evening news.

The Suburban was still adjoined to the tow truck which would drop pit at a dump on the edge of Guaymas.

"Oh my," was all I could muster from my arid throat. It was then that I spotted Teddy, Shelley, and Tracey all sobbing uncontrollably, with Craig awkwardly in the background trying to pat their shoulders and backs in solace.

"What the..." were Tina's only words. As our wide eyes met, in unison we looked down at Tina's "lucky" ring and then began scouring the area again, trying to take in all the frightening scenery.

Off to the right we saw a few of the Boise State gang huddled as if in a Final Four basketball timeout, down by two points with 21 seconds left on the clock. Matz saw us, shook his head in sorrow and motioned for us to join them.

As we neared, each of the participants was talking wildly and at the same time, trying desperately to tell us of all happenings and to explain the fire-scorched vehicle. After about 30 seconds of not being any closer to knowing what had occurred, Tina raised her hands and asked that only one person talk at a time and pointed to Barbie as the selected speaker.

Barbie had completed her narration of the incident as told and shared to her and the group by a lone *federale* police officer from Hermosillo who spoke and understood English. As I listened, my head started to spin, and I could feel the vomit pushing its way up.

There had been an old truck that had somehow been converted into a cattle car or livestock carrier. It had been dark, and the driver of the slow-moving vehicle did not have any rear taillights. The Suburban had rear-ended the small truck on the single-lane highway that connected San Carlos with Hermosillo. Police had estimated the Suburban was traveling at about 75 miles per hour on the highway when it collided with the creeping truck traveling about 25 miles per hour. The collision had been serious, but much worse was that a semi-tractor trailer was unable to avoid the Suburban that was turned on its side and stretched across both lanes. The 18-wheel tractor trailer did not have enough warning or time to slow down and had slammed into the already seriously damaged Suburban. Gasoline and oil, mixed with the tremendous impact of the semitruck, had instantly ignited all three vehicles and an explosion had occurred within tens of seconds. Three people had lost their lives that night in the horrific crash and there were two survivors, one still in serious condition and the other already treated and released. The words "death" and "dead" kept rolling, spinning, and bouncing inside my pinball action brain. Shelley's dad and Teddy's *amigo* Marcus had been in the Suburban and burned in the fiery ensemble. It was unknown whether they had been burned alive or if they had already been put into eternal rest before the flame ignited. The driver of the cattle hauler had also died at the bloody scene. Paul was in the intensive care unit at Hermosillo's largest hospital. Teddy's surviving *amigo* did not have his seat belt on and was thrown from the vehicle during the initial contact with the smaller, older truck. Reports were that Paul's pelvis was broken, a hip and a leg had several bones that were badly broken, and both arms and his face were severely bruised. The *federale* had stressed several times to his BSU audience that Paul was very, very fortunate to be among the living. At that moment I did not feel fortunate to be among the living as I could still smell the stench of burnt rubber, smoldering metal, and brutal death.

    I didn't want to bring attention to myself, but one question was eating at me.

    Biting my lower lip as fierce as I could without cutting through the skin, I tried to casually ask my question, but my shaky, timid voice was drowned out by another student's question.

    But before another student could say a word, I hung my yearning question out to face the wind and scrutiny, "How come when we called the hospital they told us that no one had been admitted?"

My Bad Tequila

Barbie took the lead with a resounding response, after first shaking her head as if disapproving of my inquiry. "Because the hospital was looking for three Americans," Barbie said. "At the time Paul was admitted, he was unconscious and had no identification on him. In fact, none of the deceased had ID on them and no one is saying why. When Paul finally awoke this morning from his partial coma, he began asking about his companions in the vehicle. The *federale* just told us that Paul couldn't remember the accident, just that there were the three of them heading into Hermosillo to find Teddy and bring him back here to San Carlos."

Barbie hesitated just long enough to take a breath and Ritchie chimed in to finish bringing Tina and I up to date. "After Paul started asking questions, it seems the head nurse started checking around and she so happened to see one of several *federales* who were called out to the accident, and he had told her of the other victims who had died on the scene. She then had her friend bring in an officer who spoke English to get as much information from Paul as he might be able to provide, and thus the vehicle was hauled over along with the sad, sad news."

I hadn't noticed that the other four mourners had come and joined our awkward circle. Teddy just stared at me with those watery and hollow eyes. I couldn't look at him and dropped my eyes as I heard sniffles and whimpers within the area, not sure if they were coming from Shelley or Teddy or both.

Tina asked the next question that had pushed its way to the frontal lobe of my brain but which I was not going to vocalize, "Are we leaving tomorrow morning, and have the parents been contacted along with Shelley's mother?"

"No and yes," came the authoritative answer from Craig, showing again that he was in charge. "I have spoken with them all and it was not a pleasant task," adding the last bit to inform and emphasize to us all of what a responsible party like himself has to go through in an unplanned catastrophe. "And no, we are not leaving tomorrow morning as there is some unfinished business and reports that the local and federal authorities would like the family and friends of the deceased to clear before heading back."

At the sound of the word "deceased," a large bawl came from Shelley that started deep in her belly, continuing up through her lungs, finding her throat, and then out her open cavity of a mouth. It was an alarming, unpleasant sound. Even a calf doesn't bawl that loud when it loses its mama.

My insides and lunch were nearly to my neck and about to spew out directly without stopping to say hello to my throat. I moved from the group, head churning, and paused at the cliff overlook before retching my partially digested food at frantic speed into the desert overhang and rock landscape that sharply fell to the sea.

After what seemed a quarter of an eternity and with not a morsel left in my empty stomach, I spit and then wiped my mouth best I could with the back of my hand. Keeping my head down and walking directly to my room, I fumbled for my key and entered the tiny, spinning room. The brown cardboard box was sitting on the floor next to the washbasin and I grabbed a Pacifico from its carton, opened it at the sink and tipped back the extra warm beer. Within seconds, I had opened three more and finished them with the same guzzling action until no barley and hops remained in the twelve-ounce glass containers.

I heard a knock and yelled, "Go away."

Another knock and then I heard Tina's voice, almost whispering through the door, "Rhet, are you okay?"

"Yes, I'm fine, now please leave me alone."

After finishing off what must have been eight or nine bottles of Mexican beer, again I threw up, this time in a more civilized manner. Stumbling up to the commode I heaved and relieved myself by forcing two fingers down into my throat. I knew what I was beginning to feel deep in my gut was bacteria from a case of bloating or overeating. Being a member of FFA (Future Farmers of America) I knew the signs and symptoms and what was causing the unrelenting discomfort: it is called enterotoxemia, an overeating disease in cows that arises when undigested carbohydrates stimulate the proliferation of bacteria

My Bad Tequila

(Clostridium perfringens type D) which produce harmful toxins in the cow's intestines. The cattle usually end up in this condition by overeating grain; I had entered it by over-indulging in barley and hops. How I could remember this I have not a clue; Sometimes I can't even think of the properties equation for water—H something, H2O, I believe, not for sure; yes, it made up about 70 percent of the earth's surface, and I was supposed to be having the time of my young life at the Sea of Cortez.

After emptying my stomach again, I knew where my next stop would find me. And perhaps the stop after that. My quickly formed strategic plan was already in full operation.

CHAPTER 12

Tequila Darkness
(Oscuridad de Tequila)

Stumbling out of the bar, I made my way sloppily across the street to the open-air Mexican liquor store and grabbed two of the closest tequilas that sat upon the lower shelf.

Dragging my body up the hill with one drunk good leg and one drunk bad leg, I finally crested the top, swerved, and curved my way across the parking lot. I was 10 feet from my room with my paper bag, now one quarter less heavy as I had already downed half of one of the 750 milliliters bottles of tequila, when a voice called out, "Rhet, Rhet, I need to talk with you."

I didn't have to look up from my focused vision of each placing step to know which beautiful body that sound exited from. "Not now, Tina, please…," I begged, sounding as pitiful as I felt.

"Babe, I really need to talk with you, pleaseeee?" she asked too politely, cancelling out my previous please.

Looking up to meet her eyes with mine, I nearly dropped my brown bag with its precious contents, tequila, my sorrowful *amigo*.

"Okay but make it fast. Can't you see I really don't feel like seeing or hangin' with anyone." I slowly spoke it more as an explanation than posing it as a question.

My key still around my neck, I set the tequila down on the cracked stoop as I knew better than to try and do more than one simple task at a time. That tequila was my out for the next day or two.

Pushing the door open, I waved Tina in before me, picked up my precious baggage, and joined her in my room.

"What's so damn important?"

"Rhet, what is wrong with you? Why are you acting this way? Why are you drinking so heavily? You smell awful."

"Well, that's a great way to start this soooo important conversation." I intentionally drew out the "so" as to irritate Tina, hopefully ending our talk.

"What the...," I stammered as I looked around. My room was nearly empty except for my suitcase, an old set of clubs, and the bright orange and blue Boise State Football travel bag lying by my cot. The scuba equipment and all the others' travel supplies and luggage had been removed. Something else was gone. A fucking bed was missing as well.

"Theodore moved everything out a couple of hours ago. He's already loaded his, Paul's and Marcus's scuba gear, and luggage onto the bus. He is going to room with Matz and Ritchie and that other guy. He told me to give you his key and that he doesn't want to see or hear from you right now."

"Why that little bastard." As soon as I had blown the words out into the air I wanted to suck them back in. "I'm sorry for saying that. I didn't mean it...I like Teddy. I can't even imagine what he is going through right now."

"I know, it's going to be all right." Tina tried to console me, but I didn't want to be consoled. I didn't want to be anything and I didn't want anything, just to have my emptiness and tequila, to share them with no one, alone in my room.

"No, it isn't going to be all right or haven't you heard? Or are you just so fucking stupid that it hasn't sunk in that three people are dead and another one of our mates is still in the hospital because of my actions?" My voice was so evil that even I didn't recognize it.

"Don't blame yourself, please Rhet," she pleaded, almost in tears. "I know you don't mean what you're saying right now and I understand."

"OHH, don't blame myself. Who the hell do you think Teddy is blaming, and I can give you twenty-to-one odds that I know who Shelley is cursing at this very moment. So don't tell me you understand." I spit the words at her and then, for emphasis, took a huge swig from my 100% agave, *hecho en* (made in) Mexico bottle.

I gulped down three more over-sized shots before wiping my mouth and letting out a, "Yum yum, *me gusta* tequila."

I unlocked the back door, which took much longer than it should have and walked onto the small patio with my nearly empty glass bottle, my only friend, held tightly. Darkness had set in and I reminded myself, "I only have two more nights in this sorry ass Mexican town and country," sounding my thoughts into words out in the open breezy air. I noticed fog had started to form and was nearly up to our motel's altitude.

"Good," I secretly thought. "This fog will hide me as I drink out here tonight," smiling for the first time since coming back from the beach that afternoon.

Faint weeping was coming from inside and I took a step sideways to look in on Tina. She was crouched on my bed, not fully in the fetal position, but close, and sobbing quietly. And once again, there was the fucking tiny blue book with the wording "Diary" sticking out of her bag.

Not wanting to hear more sounds of sorrow I stayed on the exterior side of the room and finished off my bottle. "One down, one to go," was the only thought that I could muster.

My Bad Tequila

"You'll see the true reflection of me when the tequila bottle is empty," I shouted out to the wind as I tossed the sad, angry, bottle-shaped mirror towards the sea.

I sat for a while and watched the fog slowly envelope the town, the surrounding mountains, and everything else I had been able to see minutes before.

After what could have been five minutes or it could have been an hour, I stepped back into the room and grabbed my other bottle. Tina was now quiet and appeared to have cried herself to sleep. Untwisting the fresh bottle of agave, I took a giant-sized gulp and then bellowed, "Okay, you want to talk, let's talk," while pushing roughly at Tina, intentionally pulling her from peaceful slumber.

Rico Austin

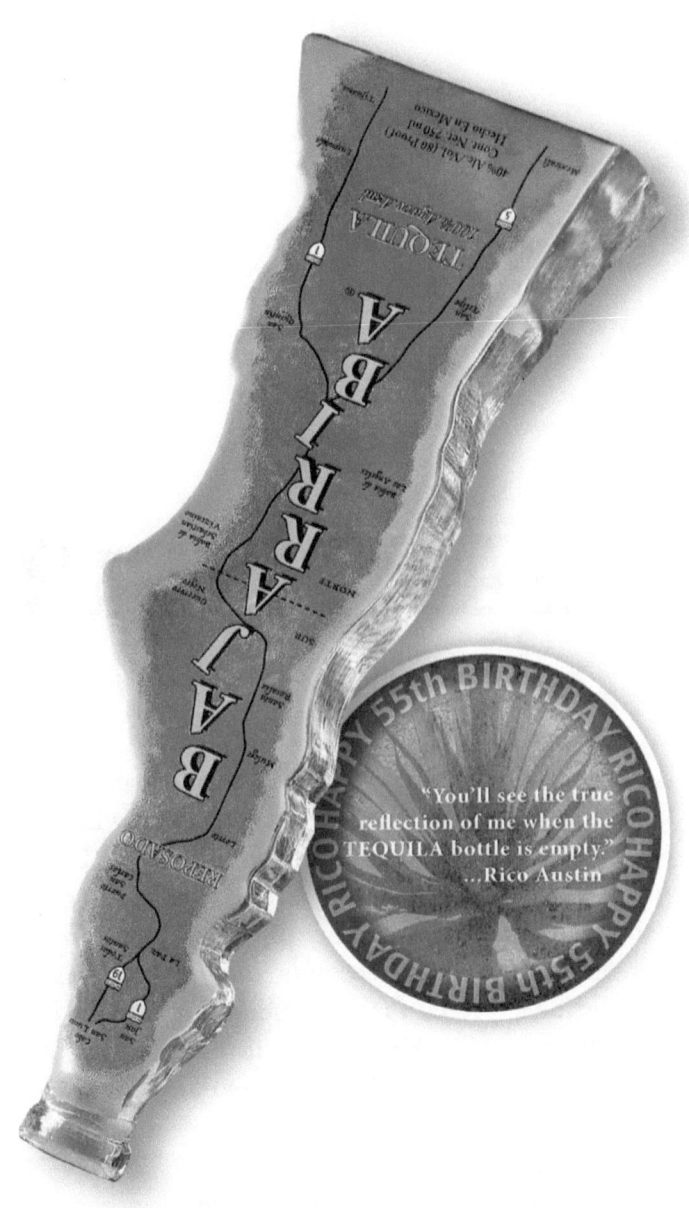

My Bad Tequila

CHAPTER 13

The Fog
(La Neblina)

"Aaugh, my head hurts," was my morning's awful beginning. Glancing around the much too day-lit room with one eye shut and the other eye wishing it could close, I noticed the back door still fully open. I was in my bed alone, fully dressed, brace and all still intact, including my toes still tucked into my flip flops. I gave my pupils one last rest for approximately 30 seconds and sat up, eyes darting as quickly as could be expected for my tequila. I spotted it by the wall, with about an inch left. Walking over to it, I stepped on broken glass that sawed right through the synthetic rubber of my flip-flop and sliced the bottom of my right foot. "Shit!" I screamed in surprise and pain, then looked down to inspect my cut.

It was then that I saw broken brown glass everywhere. My deposit was gone; I did have a pair of damaged flip-flops and a cut heel.

Blood spewed from the gash and I felt nausea as I made my way back to the cot before nearly fainting. Sprawling on the bed, I quickly wrapped my foot with part of the dingy sheet and tried to elevate my damaged foot while drifting back into a restless sleep as the throbbing pain never quite allowed a deep sleep. When I opened my eyes again, I saw the shadow of a person backing away from my patio door.

"Hello, who's there?" I beckoned a friendly welcome. The crunching of gravel grew fainter as the shadow disappeared.

A familiar agave stench filled my plugged nostrils as I raised my body from its resting spot to make my way carefully to the nearly empty tequila bottle. Next to it, greeting me, was an unfriendly reminder of the night before: a puddle of vomit resembling contaminated Weber blue was next to the pure Tequila I wanted and would have.

My imagination came alive, bursting its way through the tequila and *cervezas*, thinking how appropriate of Jimmy Buffett's "Margaritaville" and the verse "cut my heel and had to cruise on back home." My next thought was, "What in the world happened here last night?" trying to recollect the last thing I could recall.

Searching, searching my memory bank, aw yes, it was coming back to me now, there was fog last night, real fog, I was drinking tequila and was trying to wake Tina up, and, and…my mind came to a sudden halt. No more could I remember; the harder I tried, the worse my eleven pound or so ugly, hung-over melon pounded and reverted me back to all moments, minutes, and days prior to the eve before.

Blank. Blank after dark blank was in my brain; nothing still nothing. Lifting the jug to my lips I downed another large shot to ease the pain and lightly shook my head to clear the webs and wash the insides of my throat and mouth free of the vomit residue.

The last remaining bit of the precious alcohol was poured onto the gash for sterilization. I winced hard from the fiery burn of tequila that crept deep inside the wound.

This had been the second time in my life where I had obliviously blacked out. An eerie feeling engulfed me as I recalled what

My Bad Tequila

I had not remembered from the first time, as I had not recollected the happenings of a night before. A year and a few months earlier there had been a "beach party" at Humpin' Hannah's in Boise during the first part of December to help winter away the blues. Heavily advertised on most of the radio stations and flyers taped and nailed to poles, this was an event not to be missed by anyone who considered himself or herself to be "hip." Sand was to be trucked in from the Bruneau Sand Dunes in Owyhee County and leis were to be given at entry. Drink specials would be drunk. This was a gala of epic proportions.

My buddies and I had made plans to meet in shorts and tank tops at Hannah's that particular "beach party" Friday night. I had been the first to arrive and had already thrown down a couple of slow comfortable screws with sloe gin, Southern Comfort, and a bit of orange juice by the time most of the motley gang had arrived. These sloe screws were slowly screwing me out of my memory, but they quenched my thirst as Kool-Aid had years before. I drank, I danced, I talked with my pals and I drank more. The last thing I remember of that memoryless evening is telling one of my close friends I was heading to the bathroom.

My next memory conscious moment was hearing the pounding on my apartment's front door and the blurry vision of my bedroom. More pounding. I went to the door, pissed off to be roused from my rest. Standing in only my boxers and ready to vocally lambast some bastard, I was shocked to see a Boise Police Officer and what looked to be a smaller, much younger officer dressed in a Boy Scout uniform. Gaining my composure quite quickly, but still flustered, I asked, "How may I help you?"

"Excuse me, are you Mr. Rhet Austen?" the officer asked, very directly.

"Yes, I am, what is the problem?" I was now a bit uncomfortable as I realized my underwear and I were alone before a city law man and a troop boy.

"Is this your brown Granada parked out front here?" he

questioned, even though he knew it was.

"Yes, it ...What the hell happened? How did it get that huge dent in it?" I asked accusingly.

"That's what we're here to find out," he said and then added, "This is Tyler, he is an Eagle Scout riding with me today. He wants to be a police officer and help people when he is older."

I casually waved at Tyler and said, "Good luck," while focusing attention on my damaged ride and much needed transportation.

"Mr. Austen, did you go anywhere last night?"

I had a lapse, then said, "Yes, I was at Humpin' Hannah's last night with friends."

"Did you drive?" The questions were getting more difficult. "Yes, I drove to the bar, but, but I can't remember how I got home." The boy Eagle Scout looked at me like I was from another galaxy. Puzzled beyond belief, it was clear he was thinking, "How can someone not remember what they did last night?"

"Well, it looks like you may have driven home last night, hit a parked van and knocked over a stop sign down the street a couple of blocks," the officer explained. Oddly, he didn't seem irritated in the least.

The boyish Scout, on the other hand, was ready to cuff me and put me in the back of the squad car in my skivvies. Young Tyler had not yet experienced the effects of alcohol, as most likely had been experienced by his gun-toting and badged mentor.

"Wow, I don't, don't know what to say," I gulped, now almost fully understanding the seriousness of the situation but not understanding the memory lapse.

"Do you have insurance, Mr. Austen?"

"Yeah, I mean, yes, sir I do," heading back inside to try and retrieve my keys.

The officer being schooled in the art of detectivism, knew where I was going and shouted, "Your keys are still in the front door."

"What a damn idiot you are," I said under my breath as I removed the key from the door latch.

My Bad Tequila

After looking at my insurance papers, registration, and driver's license, Boise's finest announced, "Since you have insurance, I'll give the information to the owner of the van and, more importantly, a word of advice, you'd better be more careful about drinking as much as you did last night if it causes you to black out."

"Yes sir…and what about the stop sign?"

"The city will take care of it, and again, be careful. You could have killed someone last night and not even known about it."

I thanked the nice man dressed in blue and tried to thank the Eagle Scout. Tyler just gave me a look that said, "Throw away the fucking key to the cell he belongs in."

I had a feeling Tyler was going to make a name for himself as a Boise City police officer in the not too far future.

As with the car incident, I could not remember a single thing beyond trying to harshly awaken Tina. I shuddered at the thought of all the tequila I had drank, and not knowing what had taken place in the dark hours earlier.

Like the eve before, everything was again foggy.

CHAPTER 14

The Disappearance
(La Desaparicion)

The entire day was spent looking for Tina after I had borrowed a mop, bucket, and broom from Luis at the front desk. He had mixed for me some detergent along with the warm water he had prepared in the plastic, tan bucket that clung to a rope where had been a wire handle covered with thin rubber in its younger years.

Luis had exchanged the bloody sheets for a pair of clean twin-sized sheets. He was the only one I told about my cut foot. He asked to inspect my injury, but I assured him it was not too bad and that I would be all right. After all, it was on the same side as my braced leg, so the limp was not much different than it had been.

With the room swept and cleaned of blood, vomit, beer and tequila, I set out in search of my girl—Tina. I desperately wanted to ask forgiveness. After waking up to a new day, seeing and smelling all

My Bad Tequila

the filth, I wanted to start anew.

Tina was right in her assessment of the situation, in that everything would be all right.

"What was with all the blood? Was that all from the injury on my heel?" The two questions circled and then tangled in my clogged mind. "Why the fuck had I decided to settle the score with a dead worm's best friend's cousin (mescal) that of tequila?" I asked myself repeatedly that morning and afternoon while hobbling with my braced leg and cut foot throughout San Carlos.

On and off the local bus, in and out of every *cantina*, *restaurante*, and curio or gift shop. I had even ventured into the higher-end gift shop of Sagitarrio and the Arte Galleria in hopes of seeing Tina purchasing a souvenir or art for her mother, or for anyone. I had covered the small resort town on both sides of the wide divided street. My search had taken me to some of the resort and hotel bars and pools, where I would strip down to my underwear and refresh my sweaty self. All the while trying to find my *amiga*. I lost my bandage, which was removed from my damp foot at the first pool I entered. The cut grew wider and turned the pain volume up loud. I had no choice but to order margaritas and *cervezas* at each establishment during the quest for my dear girlfriend.

Stumbling out of Charlie's Rock - a restaurant/bar on the *malecon* (pedestrian seawall) overlooking the sea, I was nearly hit by a passing pickup truck. Eyes following the path of the truck, I quickly raised my middle finger and yelled something in Spanish, a bad phrase I had learned in Marsing from the working immigrants in Idaho years prior. Stopping in mid curse, I thought I saw Tina looking out the back window at me, her face wet with tears. I could have sworn it was her sitting between two Mexican guys.

"Was that Tina?" "I'm sure that was Tina, wasn't it." I played the vision I just witnessed over, and over again in my mind. Maybe the tequila and beer had messed with my eyesight or my entire head. I just couldn't be sure if I saw her or not.

It didn't make sense for Tina to be in a vehicle with the locals, did it? What color was the truck—white? red? brown? All colors seemed to run together as when not washed separately in the machine. I didn't know and could no longer see the vehicle. But my eyes had locked onto Tina, and I was certain it was her. Well, nearly certain.

Now, surer than I previously had been that Tina had been the girl in the pickup truck, this only set in motion many, many more unanswered thoughts and puzzles. "Was Tina begging me for help?" "Maybe she was being kidnapped and taken by force!" "Maybe she wanted to be with her new Mexican *hombre* and was done with me." Each thought scared me; which scenario was the scariest, I could not reason.

The hot, sweltering day turned to a cooler, humid evening and then into complete darkness. I had checked back with the hotel three times that day just to make sure Tina had not returned. I had seen most of the other students in various places during my day-long hunt for Tina; but had elected not to talk with anyone other than to ask if any of them had seen Tina. I was sure they did not want to converse with me, as most of their responses had been a very quick and decisive, "NO!"

None of the students had seemed to notice that I was limping a bit more than usual, which was fine with me. Maybe, they thought it was the tequila. Some of it probably was. Great, I didn't want to have to explain that I had sliced my foot on broken glass, in my room; this would only raise more questions and dissent in my direction.

With two more six packs of Mexican beer—Corona this time—I settled in my lonely, three-single-bedded room and drank on my patio for most of the evening. Some other students had come to sit out for their last evening and to gaze out towards the seemingly endless sea of water. I teed up a few of my used balls that I had in my old golf bag and drove them into sun just above the horizon, where each of them dove into the sea. I then limped back into my room to snore the night into morning.

I felt all eyes staring at me as I climbed onto the blue bus that had once been yellow and now sported a Porta-Potty hooked up in the

My Bad Tequila

rear. This was the end of my Mexican Spring Break holiday, and we were headed back to the frigid March wind and perhaps a skiff of snow in Boise, Idaho.

Little did I know at that time, my life would never be the same again. "It's all good until it turns bad," I would later remember.

"Crap, last one on," I thought to myself. My half-empty Corona with the lime trying to stay afloat dropped from my tanned, shaky hand. It didn't break, as it hit the rubber mats placed so strategically within the doorway to allow for all things, domestic or foreign, to bounce carelessly yet non abrasively onto the street. The bottle rolled onto the pavement which consisted of gravel sewn together with black tar next to a partially eaten tamale covered with a green salsa that was a bit too ripe. I went after my beer and picked it up, now three quarters empty as some people would say. I grabbed it up, seeing the bottle one quarter the way full. My positive outlook on life helps me see things this way.

I boarded the bus with a bit of difficulty due to the metal support brace that I fixed to my right knee. I looked at my "*amigos*," a word we had learned on this trip to Mexico, we each used it loosely – each person, place or thing that we encountered was our *amigo*.

"Sorry for being the last person."

It was 8:12 a.m., we were supposed to be gone, and on the asphalt-broken highway back to life as we knew it at no later than eight a.m. There was a silence of which I have never heard before nor have ever heard since. I trapped the bee with my thumb that had been swarming around my beer either attracted to the fruit inside my bottle or the rotten salsa that was smeared on the outside.

"Still nothing from Tina?" The words came slurred from my dry, swollen, partly scabbed lips, which had enjoyed too much sun and salty margaritas.

My question was answered by the anguished looks of my fellow Spring Breakers. Tina had not surfaced.

This is "My Bad Tequila."

Rico Austin

The End

My Bad Tequila

Now that I have your attention, turn the page.

Rico Austin

One more page should do it.

MY BAD TEQUILA

PART TWO
(MI TEQUILA MALA – Parte Dos)

CHAPTER 15

Life Disruption in Idaho
(Vida Perturbacion en Idaho)

The bus ride had been the quietest trip imaginable and by far the longest of its kind known to man. Being the last person to board I did not have much choice of where I would sit for the long haul back to Boise. There were two empty seats back-to-back in the fifth and the sixth row, so I slung my belongings into the bench seat of the closer row. For 1600 miles I chose to look at no one and nothing.

Tina had not reappeared, and I had argued with the students and Craig to wait for another hour, which we had done. The hour had come and gone. I then tried furiously to stall another hour to wait for Tina's safe arrival; it was a 100 percent disagreement by everyone else versus Rhet. I had wanted desperately to stay. But I was fund-less and friendless, and no *dinero* was coming my way in the form of loans or gifts. I had no way to stay in Mexico and search for her.

The finality of the struggle ended with the scuba diving, bus driving, trip leader saying, "Get off the bus and stay here or get your ass in a seat." That is when I had chosen seat *numero cinco* (number five) to plant my butt for the next two days.

Our longest stop of the trip was alongside Interstate 10 in Tucson, where phone calls were made to parents and loved ones. I had quietly asked Barbie to call Tina's family to tell them that Tina had not boarded the bus for the return home. Two hours later, back on the bus, there was much ado as the long-distance talks had not gone well and again more than half of the student body and all of the chaperones were in tears, some quietly and others not so quietly. We did receive some positive news: Paul was to be released the next day. His parents were expected to arrive at Hermosillo sometime that afternoon to be with their broken but healing son.

Our arrival back at Boise State University was a complete disaster. Local camera crews from the big three affiliates, ABC, CBS and NBC, were awaiting our not-so-safe return, as were carloads and carloads of families. I waited on the bus, watching from my window at the hugs, kisses, and tears being showered upon the returning students. Slowly, slowly the exhausted travelers loaded into cars, the television crews packed their equipment, and the parking lot displayed more and more asphalt until only three cars and 10 people remained.

I could tell from my vantage point which family belonged to Tina, her Italian-looking Senator father in his three-piece-Armani suit and her handsome olive-complexioned mother hiding her face in her hands. Tina's mother, peering between her split fingers, spotted me sitting alone in the bus and a brief questioned look replaced her grieving face as she dropped her hands to her side.

I looked away, probably not as quickly as I should have as I was enthralled by her beauty and the resemblance to her missing daughter. One of the other remaining families was that of Marcus. I suppose they had shown up in hopes that the horrid news was not true and that he was alive. His dad had climbed onto the almost-deserted bus and had looked at me, trembling. "Please tell me Marcus will be coming home," he said.

I could no longer hold back my feelings of loneliness and grief and softly responded, "He was a great guy." I moved from my seat and hugged Marcus's dad, both of us weeping for a few seconds until another young man, probably Marcus's brother, asked his dad, "Please come off the bus, Mother needs you."

The third family was that of Shelley's. It looked as if her uncle, aunt, mother, and sister were present. Shelley glared evilly when she saw I still remained on the bus back from nowhere and everywhere. I just stared sadly back.

I was in despair over two things, really. First and foremost was that my love was missing. Second, I was alone. No parents, no siblings, no friends had shown up to welcome me, to make certain I had arrived safely home. I had chosen to tell barely a soul of my travels to Mexico and Spring Break plans, and this was my repayment; however, it would not be my final installment.

The days following flowed seamlessly by; morning, afternoon, evening, night. Each one the same, each one different. BSU had not seen or heard from me since my departure to Mexico and would not see me in the near future. I had not called my family and had not talked with any *amigos* since that March walk from the university's parking lot to my apartment. I hadn't eaten much and had drunk very little.

This day was just like all the other days until I heard the obnoxious banging of my front apartment door. I opened it casually without asking who it might be, and four officers rushed me, throwing me headfirst into the coffee table by the couch and onto the carpeted floor.

I was handcuffed in seconds and one of the officers read me my Miranda Rights. "You have the right to remain silent. Anything you say can and will be used against you in a court of law. You have the right to an attorney. If you cannot afford an attorney, one will be appointed to you. Do you understand these rights as…"

My Bad Tequila

CHAPTER 16

Life in Between
(Vida Mientras Tanto)

Awoken by a hard slap and a punch to the midsection, I managed to open one eye. The other seemed to be swollen shut. I couldn't reach up to feel my face as both hands were tightly held behind me with a pair of metal circular rings connected by a link of chains.

"What, what's going on here?" I asked. "Why was I beaten and arrested?"

"Oh, we've got ourselves a wise guy here," was the response of a Dunkin' Donuts diner with about 35 pounds of ugly fat around his midsection and another four pounds drooping from his second or third chin.

After that came laughter from the three other officers, who were not in as bad physical shape as the sweet tooth in a uniform, but just as mentally insecure.

"I want to know why I am here and what I am being charged with," I demanded, blood dripping from my cut lip and a throbbing ache in my banged-up head.

"Killer Boy from Mexico wants to know what he's being charged with," came a new voice from behind a badge as two officers pushed me to my feet and walked me to the nearest of three carelessly parked patrol cars scarred with "Boise Police Department" on both front doors. The officer using the smart-ass verbiage was younger than the other officers and reminded me of someone. Skinny-ass kid that he was, I tried to think of who it was that had once given me that same disgusted look.

"Ah yes!" it came to me: the Boy Scout riding with the officer that morning when recollection had disappeared and left me without a night before memory. This hard-nosed, thin idiot looked to be his older brother, almost identical to the kid on the ride along after my blackout car crash. Both of their teeth had rounded edges as if tapered circularly by a slow-speed dental rasp grinder. They each had a look that said, "I hate anyone that is on the opposite side of the law" (even before conviction). I thanked my lucky stars that neither of them would be able to sit on my jury and then I gulped "hopefully," as I bent my head and lowered myself into the four-door sedan, a metal screen separating me in the backseat from the free world.

"Murder in the First Degree," was what I was being charged with, according to the officer in the front passenger seat of the squad car.

"You're kidding…you must be kidding," I sprayed the words from between my lightly spaced front teeth.

"Does it look like we're kidding?" He added, "Remember, anything you say, can and will be used against you in a court of law."

It was a short ride to the station, although it seemed to take forever as my level of panic soared and my indented, clamped wrists started to ache.

Fingerprinted, photographed, and given new dress attire

My Bad Tequila

consisting of an orange jumpsuit and open-toed rubber slippers, I made my way slowly, unbelievably, to a directed cell. After letting the shift-in-charge officer in on my financial situation or lack thereof, a court-appointed attorney gave me a welcome, if temporary, exit from my shared cell of two other "innocent-until-proven guilty" individuals. According to the bunks, there was room for one more unlucky dude.

"How are you doing, Rhet?" was his concerned, initial question.

"Not good! And I don't understand why I'm here," I responded with a choked and weak voice.

"Rhet, is it okay if I call you Rhet?" he asked and then continued without waiting for my okay. "You've been charged with a very serious crime, Murder One, for the disappearance and death of Tina Valentino."

Hearing the words, but not fully understanding the meaning, I nearly left the conscious world, as all blood left my system leaving my nerves red cell-less. I felt paralyzed.

"I did, I didn't kill anyone, especially Tina," I stammered and professed and nearly confessed. "I loved Tina. She disappeared in Mexico."

"That's why I'm here, to act as your public defender and to help you make the right plea."

"The right plea!" I said incredulously. "Didn't you hear me? I did not commit a crime, let alone murder."

"I understand what you are saying. But there is substantial evidence that says otherwise."

"Evidence, what evidence?" I demanded.

"A couple of college girls who went down to Mexico with you and the others have come forward with their own stories."

"That is exactly what they are, STORIES!" I screamed.

"Well, the city's prosecuting attorney has been working closely with the authorities in Mexico and they want you charged with murder. The girl's father, Mr. Valentino, is a U.S. Senator and has used his influence to have you stand trial here in the United States. He is a very good friend of the President of the United States who has a close relationship with the Mexican Governor of Sonora. My bet is the senator is calling in a favor, he wants this trial to be highly publicized here in the U.S. and wants to make sure you are tried and convicted. This is unprecedented. However, if I were you, I'd feel damn lucky right now as you will not end up in a Mexican prison if you are found guilty. You would serve your time here in the Idaho State Penitentiary."

"This is fucking unbelievable. Pure horseshit," I hissed quietly. I did not want to piss off my free lawyer.

My Bad Tequila

CHAPTER 17

Trials and Tribulations
(Enjuiciados y Tribulaciones)

The days following were utterly soulless; I did pushups three times daily and gave away my bologna sandwiches or traded them for fruit. Permitted to shower every third day, I looked forward to letting lukewarm water run over my body and lathering with cheap but strong-smelling soap that pushed away the prison stench for the two minutes; one hundred and twenty seconds of exhilarating time alone in a metal shower stall.

My week was broken up by the two visiting days. My dear mother would always be signed in and waiting when the 10:00 a.m. morning hour arrived. Sometimes one of my three brothers would be with her if they were able to break away from work that morning of that particular day. Numerous aunts, uncles and cousins made their way to the city and county jail that housed all waiting individuals before and during their court dates or trials. It was a welcome sight and relief to remove myself from the small cell for the larger cinder-blocked room filled with tables and chairs lined up three rows deep. However, it was also an embarrassing time and situation to be seeing the never-ending list of relatives, close and not so close. The medium-sized room and the proximity of tables made privacy impossible, but I had nothing private to discuss and all secrets were secret-less.

The trial eventually drew near and with it offers for plea deals by the Prosecuting District Attorney, who wished to make a name for himself. John Colturine was still in his late 30s or early 40s, but he had been promoted rapidly within the Boise Court System. My case was considered the most notorious around here since Claude Lafayette Dallas, Jr. was convicted of gunning down two fish and game wardens.

Colturine had been on the prosecuting attorney's team in that case but only as a junior member doing research and running out for pizza during late-night trial prep sessions. He had not received any recognition for the conviction and had been bitter, but not too vocal about it. He had decided then and there that he would do whatever it took to run the table as a respected and tough prosecutor when given the opportunity. This determination had brought him up through the justice system and had landed him the envious position of Prosecuting District Attorney, the youngest in the state, and in the most populous county, Ada. Boise was also the capital city, where headlines and notoriety throughout the state were easily found for a Prosecuting D.A.

Colturine's only negative assessment of the trial was that the prosecutors in the Claude Dallas case should have been able to get a first-degree murder conviction instead of voluntary manslaughter. After all, according to Colturine and the court documents, Dallas had shot the two officers in cold blood. Conley Elms and Bill Pogue of the Idaho Department of Fish and Game had approached Dallas regarding numerous poaching violations at his camp in southern Idaho (in Owyhee County, to be exact). Dallas' defense attorney had been brilliant and was able to shift the focus of the trial to the aggressiveness of one of the officers, Bill Pogue. The apparent issue had swayed the

My Bad Tequila

jury to convict Dallas of lesser charges: that of involuntary manslaughter and of using a firearm in the commission of a crime.

I had three or four things in common with Claude Dallas:

We both had lived in Owyhee County.

We both had been charged with the heinous crime of first-degree murder.

Both our names were cities in Texas: Claude in Dallas and Rhet in Austen. Even though I spelled it differently the pronunciation was the same.

We also both had little respect for some of the rudest enforcement staff.

This was Colturine's big opportunity to get a high-profile murder one conviction—in a case involving a senator's daughter, no less. The way Colturine saw it, there was only one person and one thing in his way—me and my confused state of not knowing or remembering what I may or may not have done.

The trial lasted nearly two weeks. Every single person who had been on the Spring Break trip the previous March and made it back alive, including Paul, was seated throughout the courtroom. I searched every bench for a friendly face, and none were found, except for faithful family members and a couple of close friends.

Each day I heard the muffled sound of Tina's mother and aunt bearing their sorrow in the way of tears and sniffles. Each day I saw the determined, "He'll pay for this every day for the rest of his life," look from Tina's father, uncle, and her dad's personal assistant, among others.

There were two extremely damaging testimonies from two girls who had been on the trip. Their stories were the reason I had been arrested in the first place; that and the fact that the person who was missing and presumed murdered was a member of a Washington D.C. family. They belonged to a cult also known as (aka) a political party machine.

The first damaging testimony was given to the court by Barbie. She gave her distorted perception of what had transpired during that ill-fated trip. Barbie swore that Rhet Austen had tried to rape her on the beach after buying her several cocktails at the Club Med. She also went on to fabricate that, "Rhet seemed to want to have sex with almost every female on that getaway," and added, "He and Tina were arguing and fighting on the last night that any of us saw or heard from poor Tina." Barbie made sure to weep a little and give a wistful look toward the Valentinos for increased emphasis that tugged at the hearts of the jury.

"Is that all, Ms. Jonstone?" Colturine asked of the rehearsed question-and-answer scenario labeled as a testimony.

"No, no, there is more, much more." Another dab at the eyes, from which I could see no moisture. The jury seemed very moved by the theatrical performance. There was no doubt in my mind now that Barbie was the granddaughter of the actor Norman Fell. Acting was clearly in her genes. Barbie continued, "Tina and Rhet were arguing about, about," she looked down and away from Tina's family as she finished her sentence. "Tina was pregnant."

Before Barbie could go any further, there was a large commotion in the courtroom as Tina's father shouted, "NOOOO" and was subdued just before reaching the defendant's table where he had his sights only on the man standing trial for both murdering and violating his daughter. Ending in pregnancy and death.

I heard the words, "Tina was pregnant" and nothing else as I went the color of a white linen sheet. The tuna melt Subway sandwich I had been treated to that morning, compliments of my defender, came upward and outward onto the polished mahogany table and a few splats hit the relatively cheap leather briefcase of my public attorney. "Order, order in the court," boomed the judge while he hammered his gavel on his bench. He then looked at Mr. Valentino with a stern warning, pointing his finger for a Perry Mason effect. "Another outbreak like this and you will be removed from the court and not allowed back in. Do YOU understand, Mr. Valentino?" The judge waited a brief moment for a response, and none came. "I am going to ask you only once more, Mr. Valentino. Do YOU understand?"

My Bad Tequila

"Yes, Your Honor, I understand," he stated in an unapologetic tone. He seated himself once again next to the sobbing Mrs. Valentino. As I was ushered out of the courtroom to be cleaned up I heard the judge announce, "Court is recessed until tomorrow morning, nine a.m. and we'll continue with the same witness, Ms. Barbara Jonstone," He again slammed gavel to wood to create a monstrous echo.

After I took a shower and changed into clean clothes my only suit was sent to a one-hour martinizing cleaner. My attorney had waited at the county jail for me and was instructed by the jailer when I was finally washed, rinsed, dressed, and ready for a privileged visit. Even though I was clean, I smelled vomit as I neared my attorney.

The stench was either from the brief ase or some of the spew had sprinkled lightly on the suit coat, pants, or shoes of my defender of the public. The odor nearly made me retch again, had I any food stored in my stomach.

I wrinkled my nose in disgust as I approached my attorney. "Sorry for throwing up on your briefcase this morning," I offered as a condolence and apology.

My attorney ignored the offering and asked angrily, "Why didn't you tell me that the victim was pregnant?"

"Alleged victim and her name is Tina," I replied in the same manner as he. "And I didn't know she was pregnant until this morning. It's the first time I had heard of such a thing. Why do you think I got sick? I was shocked."

"Why? Were you sickened because of what you had done?"

"What, what the fuck are you saying?" My temper was now beyond control management. "You think I killed Tina Valentino, don't you? Don't you?" I shook my head while letting it hang so that my chin was nearly touching my chest.

Thirty seconds went by and I blurted my rash decision to the overweight lawyer. "I do not wish for you to defend me. You are no longer my counsel."

"Oh you're firing me, is that what you are doing?" he asked sarcastically.

"Damn straight I am. I don't need you. You're ready to hand me over to the jury and the prison warden." I got up from my seat and went to the large steel door to be remitted to my holding cell. Turning back for a second, I said, "You stink. You smell like vomit, you piece of shit."

The next morning my ex-attorney was there, with briefcase and papers, welcoming me with an extension of his hand and the clean smell of soap and deodorant. He acted as if nothing had transpired the day previous.

"What are you doing here?" I politely asked as I shook his hand vigorously.

"I am your defense counsel and I am here to help you."

I chuckled as fakey as possible and said, "You help me? I don't think so, and that means absolutely no chance in hell will you remain my attorney."

We then went to see the judge, who asked me to repeat myself that I did not want and would not have this lawyer as my legal defense. After the judge made sure I knew exactly what I was doing, he looked me directly in the eye and said, "Young man, you're in enough hot water as it stands and the last thing you need is to fire your attorney. Do you have someone else in mind?"

"No, I do not have anyone else in mind. I want to represent myself."

"I am going to have to advise you strongly, please reconsider. This is murder one we are talking about," the judge persisted.

"Your Honor, I do not want this attorney nor do I want any other state-provided attorney. I want to represent myself. I have that constitutional right, don't I?"

"Okay, it's your call," he said as he shrugged his shoulders, then turned to the public defender. "I want you to stay in the courtroom at the defendant's table, in case Mr. Austen here decides he does, in fact, need the assistance of an attorney."

The attorney-without-a-client again gathered his belongings, which consisted of a cleaned and deodorized briefcase with a very few sheets of paper and notes, smiled wryly at me and whispered, "Good luck. You'll need it," as we left the chambers.

As I readied myself to thank him for his past services, he added, "Don't expect to see me visiting you in the big house." For the first time I saw true fight in this man.

Several minutes later the courtroom labeled number three was completely packed once again.

"I call this court to order." A light tap with the gavel and Colturine called the first witness of the day the last witness of the day prior.

"Miss Barbara Jonstone, is it all right if I call you Barbara?" "Yes, actually my friends call me Barbie. You can call me Barbie," she said, flirting with the fellow that had obtained a law degree and a powerful position.

"Aw, thank you, Barbara, I mean Barbie." After the slightest of hesitation and a quick 180-degree turn so that Colturine was facing me with the thinnest of smiles he finished another 180-degrees and once again faced the witness. "You testified yesterday that Tina and Rhet were fighting over the fact that Tina was pregnant."

"Objection," I stammered while scrambling to my feet. "Yesterday, Barbie testified that Tina and I were arguing. Nothing was said about Tina and me fighting over her being pregnant."

"Objection sustained. Continue on counsel."

"Isn't it true that Tina was devastated that Rhet didn't want their baby?"

"Objection," I said, this time rising without stammering. "Your Honor, counsel for the state is leading the witness."

"Objection sustained; Will the counsel for the state please not lead the witness." The judge looked at me with newfound admiration as if to say, "Kid, looks like you have been paying attention after all."

"Sorry Your Honor, it won't happen again," came the sheepish reply from the egotistical son of a bitch.

"I'm sure it won't, continue on with your witness, counsel."

"Barbie, please tell the jury what you heard on the night of

Tina's disappearance."

"Objection, Your Honor," this time with more confidence and composure in sync with my rising from the stationary, four-legged, leather chair. "We don't know if Tina disappeared that night or the next morning."

"Sustained." He took a deep breath and glared at the most prestigious prosecuting attorney in the State of Idaho.

"Um, Barbie, please tell the jury what you heard that night, where you were, and tell us the location of Tina and Rhet."

"I was in my room a couple of doors down and our back patio door was open. It sounded like Rhet and Tina were on Rhet's patio outside the room. Wait, at first, they were inside, and the door was open because I remember hearing Rhet shout, 'Okay, you want to talk, let's talk' and then they both came out onto the patio. Yes, they were definitely outside and were arguing quite loudly. That is when I decided to slip out onto the patio to get some fresh air. It was foggy that night and it eventually covered the entire motel area, I couldn't see anything. I heard Tina tell Rhet that she was pregnant with his child and, and Rhet was pissed, really pissed and he started yelling obscenities at Tina."

A sob came from Barbie and then, "such a sweet, sweet girl," with just the right amount of hesitation, then she began once more with her testimony. "Anyway, Rhet was drunk, I could hear him slurring his words and at times I couldn't even understand what he was saying. Tina was crying hysterically and then he and Tina went back into the room and the door slammed shut. I think I heard bottles breaking and more screaming, but I couldn't be sure."

"Is that all, Ms. Jonstone, oh excuse me, Barbie?"

"Yes."

"Your witness." The self-centered, cocky prosecutor waved his arm in a half-circular motion towards the witness stand.

Standing, and then approaching Barbie very slowly, I asked, "In yesterday's testimony, you stated that I, Rhet Austen, had tried to rape you. Is that correct?"

My Bad Tequila

"Yes, I think sooo." She blushed.

"What do you mean, you think so? You either know or you don't know, which is it?" I demanded an answer.

"I'm thinking, I'm thinking," she said and began to cry, this time with real salt tears.

I looked quickly at Colturine, then at the jury. I could tell both parties had their doubts, as was the witness.

"Well, can you please answer the question. Did I or didn't I try to rape you that night at Club Med?"

"I, I can't be sure, I don't know, maybe not." She dropped her head and so did Colturine, the Valentinos, as did most of the non-paying audience in the court room.

"Thank you," I walked back to my place at the long desk, feeling as if I had won the battle. I still had a war to fight.

"Would Prosecuting Counsel wish to redirect examination of the witness?" the judge asked.

"No, Your Honor," was the deflated response from the prosecutor. "Witness may step down."

Things seemed to be going much better now that I had gotten rid of the porky Defense Lawyer.

I gave a glimpse of a smile to the public defending attorney seated at our table as I strolled back to my seat. He just frowned and narrowed his eyes.

Until Mindy was called to testify on the witness stand.

"Put your left hand on the Bible and raise your right hand. Repeat after me: 'Do you swear to tell the truth, the whole truth and nothing but the truth so help you GOD?'" she was questioned while having her palm placed on the most holy scripture in print.

"I do," she solemnly swore.

"Would you state your full name and address for the court, please?"

"Melinda Jo Whitaker, I reside at 1347 East Landing Drive in Eagle, Idaho 83616."

"Thank you and Ms. Whitaker, please state your occupation?"

"I am a full-time student, attending at Boise State University."

"Thank you, may I call you Melinda?"

"Please call me Mindy, everyone does including my mother," she replied sheepishly but warmly. A hushed, shallow, nervous laughter echoed lightly through the grand court room.

"Yes, thank you, Mindy. Now, I am going to ask you some questions about what you saw and or heard on the morning of March 22nd, 1986. I just want you to tell the court and the jury in your own words what you did and did not see. Do you completely understand?"

"Yes, I completely understand," she again solemnly swore. "Were you awake at the time of your observation?"

"Yes."

"Have you ever witnessed anything else before in a court of law?"

"No."

"Would you please state to the court what you saw and where you were when you witnessed the occurrence of said statement?"

"I was in San Carlos at the Gringo Hotel and that morning I had walked over to see if Tina had spent the night with Rhet as she did not return to the room the night prior."

"Of all of the places to be at any given time, how did you come to be at this particular place at this particular time?"

"As I just said, I was concerned about Tina as she had not come home. The patio door was open, and I asked if anyone was home. I heard a noise, sounded like someone yawning or waking up. I peered into the room and saw Rhet on the bed, he looked like he was sleeping. But there was blood, so much blood on the floor and on the bed."

A loud stir occurred in the court and Mrs. Valentino sobbed aloud, "Oh my dear God." She was helped to stand and escorted by her sister to the rear entrance door.

The Judge did not slam his gavel to the wood, nor did he issue a warning to the court for continued silence. His reaction was reminiscent of 99 percent of the packed court room, disgust, utter disgust of the vivid vision planted in each of their minds.

My Bad Tequila

"Did you see anything else out of the ordinary?"

"Yes, there was broken brown glass everywhere and one or two empty tequila bottles."

"Was it one or two tequila bottles? Take your time and try to remember for the court."

Mindy shut her eyes as if trying to see into the past, into the morning of that March Day, into the room of which I had awakened without a complete memory. When she opened her eyes about 15 seconds later, she told the truth and nothing but the truth. "It was two bottles, one by the bed and another by the wall. I then backed out of the room because it looked as if Rhet was waking. I was outside on the patio when I heard him call out, "Hello, who's there?"

"And then what did you do?"

"I straddled the patio and ran."

"While you were witnessing this occurrence, did you witness anything else?"

"No, not that I can think of."

"Mindy, why didn't you report this?"

"I don't know, I just don't know. Believe me, I wish a hundred, no a thousand times that I would have just told someone that morning."

"Why didn't you?"

"Because I was scared."

"Were you scared of Rhet? Did he threaten you in any way or manner?"

"No, not really. Well yeah—maybe a bit. He's a football player at Boise State University and I just didn't…," her testimony trailed off into tears and sobs.

"Take your time, here's a tissue. Now don't worry."

"I'm okay, I want to finish this." Mindy, glanced my way but could not tolerate looking at the person that she believed murdered her friend.

"In your testimony just a few seconds ago you stated that you were concerned. Were you concerned as in worried?"

"Objection, Your Honor," I rose for the third time. "Prosecution is leading the witness."

"Overruled, I'll allow the question. Ms. Whitaker, you may answer."

"Could you please repeat the question for me?"

"Were you concerned as in worried?" the prosecutor smugly asked again, this time with more gusto and emphasis.

"Yes, yes I was concerned and worried." "Why were you worried?"

"I had heard some arguing the previous night, but…but I kept thinking things were okay. I figured Rhet had just had too much to drink. Oh, I wish, I'm so sorry," she finished by looking at Mr. Valentino as his spouse had not yet returned to the court room.

"It's okay," the prosecutor soothed as he placed his hand gently over Mindy's.

"No further questions, Your Honor."

"Defendant, do you wish to cross-examine the witness?"

"No thanks," I replied, completely devastated.

After the Judge excused Mindy from the witness chair, my eyes followed her towards the rear of the room, and I couldn't believe it. She was seated next to Craig, the bus driver, the scuba instructor, the asshole. Craig had taken her hand when she arrived back to her original seating place. They seemed to be an item. "Shit," I thought, "She has probably been constantly prodded by Craig to testify and make me look as horrible as possible."

I did know that Mindy was solemnly telling the truth, the whole truth and nothing but the truth as she had known it. She was testifying about everything I knew to be true and could remember.

The next day I took the witness stand. Whether it helped or hindered me I do not know. I told everything I could remember and tried to explain of the things I could not remember. I had testified of my cut foot to explain the blood; however, I could sense that not a one on the jury believed my testimony as no one could collaborate my story. I had looked at the Valentino parents and told them I could not

My Bad Tequila

have killed their daughter, that I loved their daughter. I only received scorned and unbelievable stares and glares. Those were the same stares and glares I received when telling the jury that I did not and could not murder Tina Valentino.

After my testimony the jury deliberated for 28 hours before deciding my fate.

"Will the defendant please stand," and continuing in the same breath, "Has the jury reached a verdict in the case of 'State of Idaho vs. Austen?'" the white-haired and round judge asked without emotion or thought due to years of bench time.

"Yes, we have," stated the Juror Foreman as she handed the officer of the court the piece of paper that held my future in print.

My blood went cold as I watched what seemed like a slow-motion scene; the officer of the court striding to present to the judge the folded note, once a free Tamarack tree in the Payette National Forest before being chopped down and convicted to life as paper.

The judge carefully unfolded the verdict and read it to himself as a smile slowly replaced a face lacking any emotion until this moment. He handed the white finished pulp back to the officer.

Carefully opening the verdict again, the lady with my life's outcome read aloud, "The Jury of the Court of Idaho finds the defendant, Mr. Rhet Lloyd Austen guilty of voluntary manslaughter."

Manslaughter = Man's laughter? I didn't hear any chuckles. My world went colorless, then black, and I was cold.

Rico Austin

My Bad Tequila

CHAPTER 18

Life Interrupted
(Interrupcion de Vida)

My new surroundings were different. The penitentiary was actually a welcome change from the small cell and the very limited exposure to exercise other than the pushups and sit-ups within my confined area.

Strange it was that growing up in farming and livestock country I never gave a second thought to the penning of animals or regulations about the size of grazing areas for cattle, horses, sheep, or goats. Now I knew why a cow tried to eat the grass on the other side of the fence; not because she thought it to be greener, but, because it was on the outside, the free side. It was on the side without barriers, without restrictions, without farmers determining their fate. I was the ram restrained from joining any ewes, tethered among many other rams in an environment where food was plentiful and provided. I was penned up like a wild young stallion in a stall where just outside the perimeter of the fence was a world where I could gallop with the wind, the mares, and the fillies. No freedom.

My prison plight was considered mild by most of the population of felons as I was only given a five-year sentence and with good behavior, I could be released in perhaps less than four years. Most of my fellow inmates had sentences of at least 10 years, some with 15, 20 and there was a fair share of life terms. None compared to the men who had received a death penalty. I had met one, only briefly. I cannot begin to understand the thoughts of a person who knows that death awaits on a certain day, a certain time and performed in a certain way. Being a prisoner on death row would be much, much worse than being an animal awaiting butchery at an Iowa Beef Processors plant. The animal, whether pork or beef upon death, most likely does not know death is coming. It surely is anxious as it has been hauled in by open-air trailers into long and winding chutes and pens much like they were designed by Walt Disney's ride-waiting planners for his theme parks. I felt for the man, knowing he awaited death as I awaited freedom. I did not feel complete sadness for him as I knew that he had destroyed other lives as his was soon to be destroyed. In Idaho, there are three offenses that allow for lethal injection: first-degree murder with aggravating factors, first-degree kidnapping, or perjury resulting in death of an innocent person. The condemned man I met had beat another inmate to death with a baseball bat and had sealed the warrant for his death.

Routine, routine, routine is to a prisoner's life as is location, location, location to a home buyer. Once in a while something would happen to break the routine, but it was rarely something pleasant. It did not matter if it directly involved you or not, it always indirectly involved everyone within the barbed wire and fencing.

Two such routine breakers directly involved me. The first was before I actually had a routine. The day I was transported to and entered the state system was the day another inmate escaped and left the system. I was the only prisoner to be bused that day from Boise to the high desert area towards Kuna, about 15 miles from the city.

My Bad Tequila

As I made my way to the electronic gates, three uniformed guards were leaving the premises. One of the guards gave me a peculiar look as I could see his brown eyes beneath his brimmed, government-issued green baseball hat. The man seemed humble, but I saw a slight twinkle and a wink as his pace suddenly quickened after our silent encounter.

I turned briefly to steal another glance at the mysterious prison guard when I was pushed by one of my three escorts.

"What are you looking at, prisoner? Your life is straight ahead, not out there!" was his boomed message to me.

Three hours later the sirens sounded as I was lying on my bunk contemplating my next not-so-great adventure. Within 15 minutes, news was traveling down the corridor from cell to cell that Claude Dallas was missing and an escape had transpired. As I was recollecting the path that had brought me into this barbed-wire hell, a thought crossed my mind: I had seen Dallas on his way out.

Unfortunately, I was not the only person thinking that same thought. I heard loud voices coming down the wide hall, then the hard click of my cell door releasing and one of two guards barking, "Austen, get your ass up, you're coming with us."

After being questioned over and over for hours about my relationship and knowledge of Claude Dallas and his escape I was put into solitary confinement for seven days and seven nights. It had not mattered that I denied knowing or having any past dealings or meetings with Dallas; the state was sure I was somehow involved. It's not often that a prisoner meets the warden on the same day as entry, but I did.

Claude Dallas had walked out at the same time I had walked in.

I never blamed Dallas for my black and isolated week-long confinement, but he was not on my direct *amigo* list. I just happened to be the poor bastard shackled and chained on the day that the notorious mountain man, labeled a killer, had inside help exiting the pen.

I welcomed the routine of my cell, my cot, and my cellmate after a seemingly endless eternity of darkness. My eyes never did quite adapt back to the daylight. Eventually I needed glasses, dark sunglasses to lessen the light's intensity. To this day I welcome daybreak even though it pains my eyes a bit. I would never want to live in Alaska, Canada or Russia during the long, cold and dark winter.

Darkness is a horrible thing.

The next routine breaker happened sooner than I would have wished or could have predicted.

Each prison within the United States has at least three main groups:

White Supremacists.

Black Brotherhood.

Hispanic Power.

I did not belong to, nor did I care to fit into, any of these inner-wall groups. There also are usually smaller, less dominant groups:

Jocks.

Intellectuals who spent most of their day reading or studying.

Schemers and super cons looking for a new way to skirt the system or make a buck by providing a needed or unneeded service or product given Federal Penitentiaries and lesser hardcore state penitentiaries like Idaho's. I was one of the few who actually had been to both a Club MED and a Club FED and within months of each other. I preferred Club MED; but I also knew my fateful night there had set the stage for my now belonging to Club FED.

Upon first entering the joint I had been on the high recruitment list of the Supremacists and had received "protection" in the yard and in the shower. These are the two most vulnerable areas within the system. At first, I gladly accepted the protection of the Caucasian tribe, but I knew that I did not belong, nor did I want to belong to any group that was filled with hatred for any race besides their own. Each of the three main groups were as prejudiced as the next. To them their race was the only race, to hell and extinction with the rest.

My Bad Tequila

The Supremacists did not take kindly to my not wanting to be initiated into their white brotherhood and I paid dearly for it. An unfair fight in the yard found me cornered by three of my previous protectors. I lasted for a few minutes and then finally was held down while a semi-dull shiv was taken to my left ear as a reminder for my nonenrolment in their suggested plan. After spending the night in the infirmary with my head bandaged turban style, I saw the asshole who had cut off my ear in the mess hall. With his back turned I walked directly behind him and stuck a metal fork deep into his back while forcing my elbow into his temple. The guards were quick to react, and I was again taken from the main prison population into solitary confinement for two days as punishment.

From those days forward I stayed close to the crowd of sport participants and involved myself in teaching some of the prisoners and a few of the guards to read and to write properly. This put me in a class where no one would bother me. The guards and the prisoners respected me for my donating time by teaching. A program with BSU was initiated during my stay and I embraced it and enrolled, earning an associate degree in sales and marketing from Boise State University. Life was manageable for over three years—thirteen hundred and eight days behind bars.

The day I walked out, away from those wire fences and cinder block buildings and into freedom, my mother was waiting for me in her white Chrysler Cordova. Waiting to welcome me back into society.

She may have been the only person on the planet who still believed me to be innocent of such a brutal crime. Me, I didn't know what I believed; the trip, the trial, time before Tina all seemed so long ago and distant.

CHAPTER 19

Football Memoirs Part 2
(Futbol Americanos Biografia, Parte 2)

Within days of release, I made my way towards Phoenix, Arizona in my Granada via Ely, Nevada. One of my brothers had kept my car in an old wooden shed behind his home and had delivered it to me full of gas, washed, and waxed. It was the best that the bronze Ford had ever looked with me as its title holder, but it started to burn more and more oil as the trip progressed. Upon entering the small town of Ely I had decided to give my poorly running but clean vehicle a much-needed rest and I stopped at the Circle K right off the highway. With snacks and soda pop in hand and my bladder emptied, I was ready to hit the road again. My car had other plans. It refused to start, and I was forced to spend the night at the only hotel with a gambling establishment. Welcome to "The Hotel Nevada."

My Bad Tequila

At seven a.m. the next day I had over $5,500 worth of chips on the table and the dealing girls had over $700 worth of chips in tips. What made the night even more incredible was when I had gained $300 in legal gambling *dinero* (money) I had asked one of the gals who was dealing cards if there was a whorehouse in town. She guided me in the direction of the Green Lantern, a house of ill repute, and told me to have fun. An hour later, after having celebrated a birthday with one of the young women and her *amiga*, I returned through those swinging doors of the old gambling hall. With $220 still in my hip pocket and a huge smile on my face, the winning streak continued right where I had left it, on that soiled green felt table with multiple tiny cigarette burns.

That night I never even pulled the covers back on the bed in which I had paid $39 to stay. The next morning my Granada was ready and waiting at the local mechanic's shop. When I was about to leave and to retrieve my car, the owner of the Hotel Nevada, having heard the dismal news about my winnings, offered me two free nights in Ely, food and drink included, if I would stay. He also volunteered to be my personal blackjack dealer. Luckily for me I had a job waiting in Mesa, Arizona and a deadline to meet.

Behind bars, I had met a guy whose brother was a proprietor of a construction company in East Mesa, adjacent to Apache Junction, Arizona. The owner's brother Johnnie and I had played softball and football together on the inside and had become good friends. Johnnie had been convicted of illegal narcotic and drug distribution, so he would be behind bars for another two years. I had met his older brother Doug a couple of times when he had come to Idaho to visit his brother at the prison encampment. Johnnie and Doug had been at the same table near my mother and me during two or three visits and we had talked briefly. Doug had told Johnnie that if I needed employment and wanted to move to Arizona, he would help me with a new start.

Arizona's law for a felon to change his or her name was relatively easy and inexpensive. The felon only needed to contact the corrections department within five days of applying for a name change and pay a small fee for administrative costs. A new life awaited me in the harsh climate of the Sonoran Desert, where everything alive either pricks, sticks, or bites you. Rattlesnakes, scorpions, coyotes, bobcats, tarantulas, wild javelinas, and Gila monsters welcomed me. I embraced these dangerous, wild animals in the open desert of Arizona more than I had embraced the more dangerous, wilder animals in the closed confines of Idaho.

Working for Doug was good. I had a checking and savings account once again, and after six months of working many hours of overtime and stashing money into the bank, I no longer needed to sleep on the couch in the front room of Doug's one-bedroom apartment, which he had so graciously offered me. After another half year of physical labor, I started thinking heavily about returning to school to obtain my bachelor's degree in business administration as writing and journalism no longer seemed the correct route for me. A business degree would be the ticket to a more successful environment, so I enrolled in a private school owned by the Baptist Church, Grand Canyon University. GCU was the home of the Antelopes since it originally was located in Prescott, Arizona before moving to Camelback Road near Central Phoenix.

I took a part time job as a waiter near the school. Even though I now had a new name, I still had to answer the questionnaire truthfully on each job application I filled out when asked whether I had been convicted of a felony. Voluntary manslaughter did not look very inviting on an application; but jobs were plentiful and applicants few, so a little honesty struck a fine accord with potential bosses and managers. That and I had received an excellent recommendation from my previous employer.

Grand Canyon University was a 180-degree world of difference from the joint. The school was approximately 70 percent female, of which 50 percent or higher were extremely attractive and friendly. The prison had been 100 percent men who were mostly butt ugly and none too friendly. GCU, being a Christian school backed by the Baptists, had classes such as "The New Testament" and "The Old Testament"

My Bad Tequila

that were required before being allowed to take advanced courses. Each semester "Chapel" was mandatory for at least 20 sessions. At first, I saw it as a required reading or course, but as the first semester continued I looked at it differently. I began to eagerly await this hour of singing and praising the Lord. It was exhilarating and I met a lot of NICE innocent girls with young hard bodies. This ended up being a very physical and rewarding course.

At the beginning of my second year at GCU in late August an announcement was posted of about American Football tryout for a sister learning institution in the United Kingdom. Eight universities in England had an American football program in place and each university was allowed to give two scholarships per year that included all tuition, books, meals, a dorm room, transportation to England, return back to the states and a semi-moderate spending allowance.

Three British coaches had made the trip across the pond to find two candidates for their team in exchange for two soccer players, or, as they say "footballers," to play for the Antelopes at Grand Canyon U.

I was not the fastest or the strongest at the tryouts, but I was the hardest-hitting fellow on the grass, and I leveled anyone at any time given the open field opportunity. My knee had been completely rehabilitated by the constant stretching and lifting while in prison, which I had continued upon my release, so no questions were raised about previous injuries. The coaches were impressed, and I let them know of a previous college team I once played for, so that had sealed my journey to a faraway land where the masses speak English but not correctly in my book and with a hard-to-understand accent. The coaching Brits had chosen me for defense and had chosen a tall lanky lad from Nebraska for offensive reasons. The Cornhusker farm boy could catch, and he could run. Luke Summler was every bit of six-foot-five inches tall and weighed possibly 180 pounds when soaked. The two of us became fast friends with each other and with our new English teammates.

I was thrilled to be practicing football again, to have mates again. My past was so far behind me I might never have to see it again.

My mind drifted back to the green turf I had once stepped and ran upon. That was the end of my college football career in the states. Luckily for me I was here in England at Stoke-on-Trent in Staffordshire, and I would be playing in more collegiate games.

Our team went undefeated for the season; four teams were in the playoffs. We, the Staffordshire Stallions, were matched up with a team, Leicester, whom we had beaten severely earlier in the season. Our first playoff game was right before Christmas and during the holiday school break. Luke and I were missing home and the coaches had given us the go ahead and the tickets for the visit. The championship game would be after the first of the new year and we both would be back for the big game.

Luke and I never returned, for our beloved Stallions lost by a mere two points to Leicester. Three of our starters got hurt during the first half and two of the starters were on American soil instead of on the muddy playing field.

Both of us Americans were sick about the news, angry with ourselves that we had let our mates down. We had given up a chance to be a part of something special—extra special—that of a Championship Team. Undefeated champions are rare and we would not see that rarity nor feel that sense of perfection only a true, undefeated champion can sense.

We had let our English blokes and beer buddies down. All the evenings we had spent together in the student union putting away pint after pint away disappeared. The only solace Luke and I received was by talking through the many memories and stories. We mentioned to each other time and time again about the one rule that stuck so vividly into our minds. "Good American Football Players DO NOT Drink Before a Game." This rule made sense to us, but to other brothers with the peculiar accents it literally meant "before a game," as in right before game time. At Boise State we were not allowed to drink two days before a game, but here things were different: not better, not worse, just different. It had been a blast and now it would be over, forever.

We weren't going to miss the crowds, because there were no

My Bad Tequila

crowds. Our fans rode with us in the bus to the game, mainly girlfriends and wives, and heavy petting as well as making out were not uncommon scenes while riding in a yellow bus to a green field that would soon be brown and muddy. At other times the team or the university would not have a bus available, and we would all cram into cars making the crowded ride to an away game.

To this day, I often think of what could have been if we would have stayed just a little longer on that large island. I do have one self-indulging record in the books. I am still the oldest American to play college football in the United Kingdom. What a fantastic memory playing for the Stallions. I just can't seem to get away from the horse mascots or to let it go.

I did see my former coach from BSU, Coach Mass, years later when I was living in Scottsdale, and Coach was living in nearby Tempe, where was the head defensive coordinator of the Arizona State University Sun Devils. One day I finally got up the courage to go down to the ASU stadium, entered the elevator at the stadium, and went to the sixth floor, where his office overlooked Devil field.

I rapped lightly on his open door and when he looked up a big grin covered his face. "Well, I'll be. Austen, come on in and have a seat." The welcome was much different than I had been expecting.

My first term of business was to apologize for losing the Vandal game for the Broncos. My apology was accepted, and I was told to no longer worry about it.

Coach Mass did and had forgiven me and he told me the story of how "my" particular play had gotten him noticed and promoted within the ranks of college football quite rapidly.

He then explained the road that had brought him to be a defensive head coordinator in the desert and gave me a lot of the credit. He said the exposure he received from the new blue turf the following two years after the devastating loss and how he had handled the strawberry-blond 165-pound kid from Snake River Valley had done a lot to further his career. His telling me to hit the road right away, no team meeting, nothing, had set the precedent for him as a coach who would not put up with any antics on the field or off. He was labeled a fine coach with little sympathy for those who make mistakes.

"Coach, we both know you have a heart," I said. "I know you reacted out of emotion and pressure from Sorensen."

"Let's keep that between us, shall we?" he asked. "I'm glad to see you finished your education after whatever happened in Mexico."

"Coach, I really don't know what happened in Mexico. But I'm glad that it's all over."

We continued to talk, and he offered me two tickets in the loge section to sit with all the coaches' wives for the four remaining home games of the season. Those seats were great, and they came with free food and drink. I was asked over and over about the incident that led to the turf color change. There was however, one tale that they would never know the complete outcome of.

The next year Jake Plummer would arrive at ASU and a whole new set of problems arose for another Idaho-raised kid in an even more media-driven market than Boise. Seems Plummer was destined for a horse mascot, as was I; he would later play for the Denver Broncos and then disappear from football and the sports page.

One of the several things I remember about Jake is when I occasionally ran into him or saw him out at a nightclub; he was always with his best *amigo*—Pat Tillman. They were teammates while playing college ball at ASU and both were drafted a year apart by the Arizona Cardinals where they would continue to be teammates while playing professionally.

Pat Tillman was one hellava football player and is an American hero. He was never about money, as was proven twice: Tillman turned down a five-year, $9 million contract offer from the St. Louis Rams out of loyalty to the Cardinals; the second time was in May 2002, eight months after the September 11, 2001 terrorist attacks, when after completing his contract obligation of the remaining fifteen games of the 2001 season, Mr. Tillman turned down an offer by the Arizona Cardinals of $3.6 million over three years to enlist and serve his country in the U.S. Army.

My Bad Tequila

I believe when Pat was killed by friendly fire on April 22, 2004, while fighting in Afghanistan, it affected Jake Plummer much more than most people realized. Jake, then a Denver Bronco after being signed as a free agent in 2003, had his best year season to date, ending the season with a 91.2 quarterback efficiency rating. Jake's life in 2004 was similar to a rollercoaster ride with the death of his former teammate and one of his closet *amigos*. It was also the year he surpassed or broke some of the former Broncos QB John Elway's passing records. The NFL made a poor decision with Plummer, as did the U.S. Government when it lied to Tillman's family about how he died. On Sunday, September 19, 2004, all NFL teams wore a memorial decal on their helmets in honor of the late Tillman. The Arizona Cardinals continued to wear this decal throughout the 2004 season. Plummer, who was playing for the Broncos, made a request to wear the decal for the rest of the season, but the National Football League turned him down. The NFL (No Fun League) would not grant this simple act of loyalty and honor of an American Hero, Patrick Daniel "Pat" Tillman, RIP (Nov. 6, 1976 – April 22, 2004) because Plummer's helmet would not be uniform with the rest of his team.

Bullshit at its purest.

Author - Rico Austin at Staffordshire University, UK as a Stallion

Rico and fellow American & Amigo, Matt in England

My Bad Tequila

CHAPTER 20

A New Life and Name
(Una Vida y Nombre Nueva)

I met my wife Presley in the 'hood—my neighborhood. She was my next-door neighbor and met me right after I purchased the home upon having it constructed. She was of Norwegian descent, from the lakes of Minnesota and she had a strange accent, like the actors in the film, "Fargo," only a bit more real.

Life changes quickly as does fortune, both kinds of fortune, good and bad. Fresh from a six-month paid training stint with a large tire manufacturer, I was on top of the world. Having earned an MBA from Thunderbird, School of Global Management, (formerly Thunderbird, The American Graduate School of International Management), I had been offered a position with an international firm that produced and marketed tires of all sizes. I was recruited for sales of the large earthmover-type tires because of my background in construction and farming. When it had come time for interviewing I had become extremely nervous as I figured the question was coming: "Have you ever been convicted of a felony?" But it never came, and with resumes and cover letters as the preferred hiring method I was never asked to fill out an application. Next thing I knew I was in Greenville, South Carolina going through an intense sales and product training class that had me traveling all over the United States and into Mexico. The International master's degree required graduates to have at least two languages, one of which was English, of course. My studies had gone well at T-Bird and I had made some close friends, some from influential and wealthy families. My two years earning my master's degree helped make up for the almost four years I had been behind bars. The campus was similar to a Scottsdale resort with swimming pool, palm trees, a first-class restaurant that served many ethnic foods, and a pub. The Thunderbird Pub was open seven days a week and into the wee hours of each morning. Music blared and students from all over the globe shared stories of home and of their travels to the far corners of the earth. I learned of faraway places and people of which introduction had never shaken my hand. Listening intently to these students' tales I had to be close-mouthed about my own private history and never mentioned my travel to Mexico, lest I slip while sipping on a libation.

  My admittance at Thunderbird had occurred because the Dean of Business at Grand Canyon University had liked me as a student, as president of the marketing club, and as an athlete representing GCU in England. Business Dean Don Sheriff, RIP, was a kind, generous man and also had obtained his doctorate degree. He had seen potential in me and noticed I didn't seem to have any family or close friends other than an older girlfriend and my Nebraska football mate. The great Dean and Doctor Sheriff helped me get grants and student loans and had convinced me to join the marketing fraternity of which I became president. Thanks to his support, had won the distinguished honor of "Future Business Executive of Arizona," competing against the best business students in other Arizona public universities, including ASU, U of A, and NAU, as well as the state's smaller community and junior colleges.

The older girlfriend had been a steadfast pillar in my life. I had met her snow skiing in Telluride, Colorado a couple of winters prior. The Phoenix Ski Club, of which we were both members, had taken two busloads of skiers to Colorado for a four-day trip called Arizona Days.

I had been apprehensive about taking another long bus ride as my last long bus excursion had led to the end of many lives and the destruction of mine. But this trip had been a hoot and I had started dating a platinum blond executive of a major U.S. company, who helped me immensely through my undergraduate and graduate school. After graduation from Thunderbird our lives had come to a crossroad as she was transferred out of state, and I had no idea of where I was to land after training. Neither Tina nor prison were ever mentioned or discovered.

Upon successful completion of my intense and demanding job training, I was offered a choice of two destinations: Salt Lake City or back to Phoenix. I made my decision based on the weather when presented with the choice. It was cold, the first week in December, so I opted for the "Valley of the Sun." Had it been May, June, July, or August, then my life would have unfolded in the city by the Great Salt Lake and Mormon Tabernacle.

I had saved enough cash for a down payment and had started looking for a home to purchase. My realtor was patient with me and I eventually found the perfect two-story home, in the midst of being constructed, in a gated subdivision with a community pool and hot tub. This place was everything I had dreamed of. It was MY first home, and it was going to be all mine, except for the money owed to the bank. This was where I met Presley, first as friends, and then as lovers. Several of my *amigos* had told me I would have to get married or move if I dated my neighbor. I did both, moved first, then relocated back to Arizona and hitched my post.

My life had settled down and I was so very fortunate to be able to do some things that other *amigos* would never get to do, such as take a ride in the Goodyear Blimp, hike the Grand Canyon alone, and attend incredible functions with *amigos* such as a Super Bowl. I also got to witness in the flesh as the Arizona Diamondbacks won four World Series Games over the New York Yankees in a drawn out seven-game series and in the bottom of the ninth. I was even asked to appear on another episode of Baywatch after my debut as a drug lord on a yacht opposite David Hasselhoff aka "The Hoff." All this fanfare was terrific, yet an old memory haunted me and tugged at my mind most every night as I tried to rest my body and soul. Living a life that had sketchy details for a period—at best—was constant work. I tried to push it aside as if it never happened, but each time it processed itself to the front of my consciousness. I had read somewhere, or perhaps had heard it in prison, that if you believe something long enough—even something not true—eventually it becomes reality and truth. I hoped it could work for me, but in the opposite direction.

After a few years of a bad memory constantly nagging at me, I went to my spouse and told her I wanted to explore a place in Mexico that was beautiful and on the water. The opportunity had given itself to me as we had discussed purchasing a condo, or perhaps a second home, on the beach in Mexico. *Puerto Peñasco*, or Rocky Point as it was called by gringos, had been the obvious choice. It was only about a four-hour drive from the Phoenix metropolitan area and on the Sea of Cortez. I had talked with friends about the viability of purchasing property in Rocky Point and most of their answers concurred: it was overpriced, there was too strong a drug influence, too many wild Southern Californian and Arizonans because of the proximity, and it was at the mouth of the Sea of Cortez, which is not the bluest or greenest water of the Cortez as an occasional diaper or soda can was spotted during snorkeling or diving trips.

But secretly my plan was in place—to return to San Carlos and try to find the truth about Tina and about myself.

My Bad Tequila

Rico wearing knee brace while skiing in Telluride, Colorado

CHAPTER 21

San Carlos – The Truth
(San Carlos – La Verdad)

August of 2005 was hot and humid like any other August in Scottsdale. I had just purchased my first Harley Davidson from Buddy Stubbs dealership in North Phoenix for the *viaje* (trip) to south Sonora. The reason I had chosen this particular dealership over all the others in the Phoenix metro area was that I was a huge fan of Buddy Stubbs.

When selecting a bike, there were several dealers that I could have gone to, such as Superstition Harley Davidson in Mesa, Hacienda Harley Davidson in Scottsdale, or several others that offered the same great American bike, but…Buddy Stubbs was the first Harley distributor in the Phoenix area. In business since 1966, he had grown to three Harley Davidson dealerships in Arizona. He also worked as a motorcycle stuntman in Hollywood and was a motorcycle racer. I had

My Bad Tequila

visited the "free of charge" motorcycle collection at his stores, with upwards of 300 bikes. Japanese motorcycles were nowhere to be seen. Buddy refused to own any due to a long-standing hatred of the Japanese, stemming from huge losses in sales he sustained when Japanese motorcycles invaded our shores over 40 years ago. At Buddy Stubbs, you could see some of the rarest, most highly collectible motorcycles anywhere. They were all running, all road worthy and all for sale. So, if you had enough *dinero* to satisfy the motorcycle stuntman and businessman, then you could become the "Easy Rider." My selection had been a black pearl Road King Custom, the perfect bike for my discovery trip. The timing was perfect, as I had booked two tickets to the Oprah Show for my wife and her girlfriend. Presley was as big a fan of Oprah as I was of Harley Davidson, so I gathered my frequent flyer mileage together with enough to produce two coach seats to Chicago O'Hare. I then booked them a room at the Palmer House, a Hilton Luxury Hotel in downtown Chi Town. Anytime I could throw business at a hotel, I tried to toss it Hilton's way. I admired Conrad Hilton and his perseverance in building his accommodations empire. While in prison (pretending to be a famous guest at the Waldorf Astoria) I had read "Be My Guest," the autobiography of Conrad Hilton and the transition he had made through life, from an unspoiled young man riding to school on horseback in the rugged New Mexico Territory to being married to Zsa Zsa Gabor and living in Hollywood. The man had lived and created a dynasty through hard work and determination. I wanted to have that same determination as Conrad; I believed down deep I had the moxie. For instance, the hardest part had been obtaining the two tickets to Oprah Winfrey's daytime show, but after several phone conversations and calling in some owed favors, the passes had come through and my wife was in ecstasy; she was going to see her hero. I could see some of my hero, Mr. Hilton, come forth in me if I looked closely and deeply.

By sending my wife to Chicago I was accomplishing two feats: providing a much deserved and overdue gift to Presley and taking the focus off of my Mexico trip. I concentrated on talking about

Chicago—the shopping, the girlfriend time and, of course, Oprah. To add to the excitement, I purchased the O magazine for Presley as a constant reminder of her upcoming vacation.

At the end of the first week in August we said our *adioses* and goodbyes, Presley destined for Illinois by way of clouds and anticipation, and I headed for Mexico by way of broken asphalt and destroyed dreams.

The constant rumble of the engine and the wall of heat made for a dual threat of turning back after reaching Green Valley, just south of Tucson and north of Nogales. I pulled over at a restaurant to cool off, get something to eat, and forget about going condo and corpse hunting. While parking my bike I spotted a sign on the adjoining business, a hair salon, that read "Tina's Place." A cold shiver ran through me as an eerie, old feeling engulfed my being. I mounted my new Harley and headed for the Mexican border.

T E Q U I L A T E Q U I L A T E Q U I L A T E Q U I L A
T E Q U I L A T E Q U I L A T E Q U I L A T E Q U I L A T E

As I turned the unfamiliar corner that had been familiar nearly 20 years ago, the words TEQUILA swam together as a steady pounding wave in my head. It was the corner where *Ruta* 15 (route 15) continues on into Guaymas, then down to Mazatlán and still further south. The corner where vacationers, partygoers and outlaws veer to the right. The corner where SAN CARLOS is painted high on giant white rocks across a rugged mountain sparsely covered with cacti blocking the sea. The corner where pleasure or pain might exist with that slight turn to the right.

The roaring of my Harley calmed and the calm of Cortez' sea roared.

Riding slowly through the resort town I took special care to try and notice each person, place, or thing. Little had seemed to change until I neared the marina and Tetakawi Mountain, where oversized homes were sprinkled heavily on the entire hillside which enclosed the

My Bad Tequila

bay and safe harbor.

Rounding the back side of the mountain named aptly after the upside-down view of goat teats, another grander marina had made its way through progress and brilliantly colored mansions line the mountains and the white cottony beaches. The airstrip from the film Catch-22 was nearly invisible except for a cleared path: most of the asphalt had been taken either by films buffs looking to closet a chunk of Hollywood or by locals wishing to reuse sewn tar and gravel for who knows what.

My memory lane tour ended at what had once been the Club Med, now christened Paradiso. The guard shack was abandoned, the cobblestone entry was missing cobbles, and the grounds were unkept, but the buildings were still standing. As I walked into the lobby, where years before there had been laughter and noise now there was sadness and silence. I relived the moment when Teddy had fallen from the truck, the topless girls near the pool, the music, holding tightly onto Barbie, hearing her scream into the night, the sting of the jellyfish, the taxi ride back to the hotel, and lastly the reunion with Tina's body and smile. And then came the pain.

I needed a place to stay, and I needed tequila like I had not needed it for nearly two decades.

Cruising back through San Carlos I went to the edge of town and pulled into the Fiesta Hotel. At the front desk they made sure I understood there was not a phone nor a TV in the small room. But it did face the sea, was on the beach, and had an onsite restaurant and bar just steps outside my room.

Tossing my backpack onto the bed, where a mattress had been laid upon a concrete structure resembling a bed frame, I quickly put on my swim trunks, waded into the salt water, and body surfed in the waves. I then used the long, green, cracked hose to remove or rearrange the sand that accumulated in my shorts, hair, and ass.

Showered and now wearing wrinkled shorts and a lighter print shirt I went into the Fiesta Bar and ordered a margarita *con sal* (with salt) and spoke with the friendly bartender in Spanish. I asked about real estate, condos and the weather. The bartender and I became closer friends the more tequila and margaritas I drank. It was so fucking "tequilalious." The more I drank, the more I wanted to drink and the more I drank…

An all-too familiar, yet unfamiliar pounding of the temple angrily greeted me along with the bright sun streaming into my uncurtained room. "What had happened last night?" I remember being in the bar, talking with Juan, I think it was Juan or Jose or? Oh, and I had struck up a conversation with a pretty young Mexican girl sitting alone at a table watching the waves collide gently with the sand, and, and…

"Fuck me," I half shouted, realizing that I couldn't recall some of the previous night. I didn't remember leaving the bar, didn't remember coming to my room, didn't remember lying down on this rock-hard bed.

I was beside myself with anger at having lost track of space and time once again. The last time this had happened to me was the last time I had seen the young girl I had once loved, and it had cost me nearly four years of my life. It had changed several people's lives, none for the better. Had I not learned, or had I forgotten?

Not wanting to waste any more time, I quickly scanned the room for anything that might give me a clue as to what had happened. I was naked. My swim trunks were wet and lay on the floor. Two towels were strewn on the only chair and I had light sand all over my body. "I must have gone swimming in the sea," was my hopeful conclusion. Then I gasped! I gasped for air, I gasped for life as I spotted the small sundress lying at the foot of the bed. "Hello," I called in the direction of the *baño*. "*Hola*," I yelled again in hopes of getting a response. Nothing and no one was in the room, in the bathroom, or on the balcony.

Not wanting to waste any more of the day I hopped up from the damp and sandy bed and tried to shake the scare that ran so deep into the depths of my soul.

I could not scrub hard enough to cleanse myself of the shame

My Bad Tequila

of possibly cheating on my wife and even more filthy, the fear of what gruesome act I might have done to the girl who had befriended me so quickly *anoche* (last night). After showering I looked closely at the ear that had been partially removed and reattached while serving my stint in the Idaho pen. "Why, oh why, did you start drinking tequila and margaritas?" I whispered madly into the mirror, wondering if I were somewhat insane or if I were to be permanently tormented by Mexico and its national drink—tequila. Tequila: it made my mind go blank; my memory halted when it touched my lips and my inhibitions died when tequila found her ugly way back to me.

I screamed and banged my head into the already slightly cracked mirror, sending slivers of silver-backed glass onto the old, brown-tiled floor and into the small beige-stained basin. Drops of deep scarlet blood fell to the basin and so quickly I held a cloth to the crown of my head to stop the flow.

Feeling depressed, I climbed back into the shower, this time just letting the water fall upon me. Head bowed and arms to my side I gave total submission to the stream. "What on fucking earth was I thinking coming back to this town that had haunted me for nearly 20 years?" I questioned to the new man who I thought I had become. I wasn't an evil person—was I? Perhaps being born a Gemini was a curse of constantly fighting evil twin against angel twin. I believed in GOD, I believed in Jesus Christ as my Savior, and I tried to follow the Golden Rule of, "Love thy neighbor as thyself" or "Do unto others as you would have them do unto you." And yet here I was in a tiny hotel room alone, distraught and possibly facing another felony. Because of what? Because I had not learned from my past mistakes. "My Bad Tequila" was still following me. Or had it just returned?

Taking every bit of internal fortitude I had, I put on my clothes, picked up the dress, wrapped it inside one of the towels and put it in my saddlebag.

I would continue with this trek and at least make a concerted effort of looking at a few condos before blowing out of town and back to the north side of the border. My first stop was San Carlos Beach

Realty, which had a few vacant lots and a couple of overpriced homes. Early afternoon had come, and I decided to stop at Barracuda Bob's next to the marina as I remembered this spot from years before; however, it had been closed that day Teddy and I had stopped in. The place was now semi-packed with old *gringo* sailors swapping tales and a few *amigos* with their laptops out, enjoying the free Internet service to get caught up on emails to family and friends in the states or Canada. All the tables were taken, inside and outside, so I asked a young man in his mid-to late-thirties who was banging away on his laptop as if trying to meet a deadline for a story if I could share a portion of his table and the chair that looked available. He told me to knock myself out, so I put my helmet in the seat as a territorial marker. I ordered a quick snack and an iced coffee to cool my parched throat and fight off the drowsiness caused by the extreme heat. I overheard one of the sailors mention a new condo development called Bahia Delfin (Dolphin Bay); he was saying one of his *amigos* had bought a place there at pre-construction pricing and that the builders were Americans from Tucson with an excellent reputation for quality and completion. He said it was situated on one of the most beautiful beaches in the Mexican State of Sonora. I waited for the name of the beach as the grey-haired man rubbed his forehead, trying to jar the word he needed to his mouth. "San Francisco Beach, that's it."

    A few of his *amigos* shook their heads and one of them said, "Yes, I believe that's the same beach where Pillar Condominiums are located. Burl Ives and his widow have or had a place there, very quiet and secluded."

    Upon hearing the name of the world-renowned singer, Burl Ives, my mind was sidetracked for a brief moment. "If Burl Ives had lived there it must have an incredible view; the singer of "Frosty the Snowman" and "Rudolph the Red-Nosed Reindeer" could have chosen anywhere to have a vacation home and he chose here. "I would have pictured him living at the North Pole," I mused quietly as I returned back to Mexico from the distant winter wonderland.

    Having heard news of a reasonably-priced condo on the beach

My Bad Tequila

I briefly let go of the new worries I had developed as excitement rushed in and pushed the concern out. After gobbling down my tasty sandwich, I waited for the opportunity to invite myself into the conversation and ask where I could find this new development. I was given instructions and directions to a small shopping mall behind a Pemex gas station and there I would see the signage of *Bahia Delfin*. Pulling into the new strip mall and seeing the sales office, a bit of adrenaline hit me or—maybe it was the iced coffee, as I was feeling much better about everything. There had to be an explanation for the dress in my room; I half chuckled to myself for added conviction.

I opened the door and a bell jingled announcing my arrival. Out came a gorgeous, dark-haired girl in her late teens or early twenties. I went weak and turned pale as I briefly had or thought that I had seen a ghost. This girl resembled Tina so much it was scary.

"*Hola*, is everything all right, *señor?*" she asked with genuine concern.

"Uh, yeah, um, yes everything is okay, I just thought I recognized you for a second. You remind me of someone." I stammered while trying to regain my composure and color.

"Oh yes, I've been told that a few times, that I remind people of someone."

"Well, I'm here to find out about the development going in near here. Do you have any material or information?" I asked, trying not to stare too intently at this girl.

It was then that I noticed the silver necklace hanging from her delicate tanned neck. On it was a ring, the ring of the two dolphins, identical to the one I had given Tina so many years ago. Afraid to ask, but not able to contain my suspicion and curiosity, I asked her where she had gotten such a beautiful necklace with the ring attached.

"*De mi madre*, sorry I meant, from my mother."

"Oh no, don't apologize, I prefer to speak Spanish. *Yo necesito hablar y practicar*" (I need to speak and practice). *Y como se llama?*" (And what do you call yourself?)

"I was named after my mother."

I held my breath and waited for the name.

"Anita, pleased to meet you," she said, offering her hand. "And what is your name?"

I heaved a heavy breath, took her hand in my trembling hand and said, "Rico Austin, *mucho gusto*," (glad to meet you) without much warmth and with tremendous disappointment.

"Well, I kind of was named after my mama. She and my papa, when they were young, liked to play Scrabble, so she named me while playing with letters. A N I T A is A T I N A spelled backwards. The first letter is of my papa's last name and my mother's name was Tina."

I started crying right then and there. Not tears of child support back payments, but tears of my baby, my dear baby.

"*Que* (what), I mean, what is wrong?"

"Nothing is wrong, my dear child, everything is just fine," I told her while pulling off the handkerchief I had wrapped around my neck to dry my eyes and blow my nose.

"Is there somewhere we can go to talk?" I asked my confused and unknowing daughter.

"Well, if you are interested, we can go look at the property where the condos are being built," she responded, quite unsure of whether she should be alone with this over-emotional man she had just met.

"Yes, yes, that will be great," I said, trying not to sound too eager as to not frighten Anita any more than she already had been.

I wanted to make her a little more comfortable, so I volunteered to follow her on my bike.

We drove south from town back towards Guaymas, made a right turn near the estuary and continued down a broken asphalt road that badly needed all the potholes repaired and filled.

The property was magnificent. The condos were designed in a V shape, so all of the units had a perfect view of the white soft beach and the blue Sea of Cortez. There were three sections of Vs and then a lone set of condos on each end, which if put together would form another V. The placement of where some of the beginning buildings

My Bad Tequila

were started and others were chalk marks drawn out to show where the condos would be built.

I tried to contain my excitement about the discovery of Anita, however, I could not restrain myself from asking questions. "Does your mother live near here?" I carefully threaded the question as if putting a fresh spool through an eye of a needle.

"*No, mi mama es muerta*," (No, my mother is dead), she replied in Spanish without thinking, as a sadness slowly replaced the seemingly never endless smile.

"Oh, *lo siento*, (so sorry), Anita." I touched her arm so slightly with the touch of a longtime friend.

"*Gracias*, it has been a few years now. She died when I was 12 years old of breast cancer." She reverted to English.

Not wanting to continue the sadness of Tina's daughter I mentioned how the view of the sea was lovely. We marveled at the pod of dolphins swimming not more than 30 yards from the white sandy beach. Half of the condos would face Miramar, a *gringo* subdivision of Guaymas, and the other half would face Tetakawi Mountain and part of the town of San Carlos that jetted out towards the sea creating a bay between Miramar and San Carlos. As slowly as her sadness had arrived, the happiness again crept across her face.

We walked closer to the sea to where a seawall of concrete and rock had recently been built, and then onto the virgin beach. I decided that this was the perfect place to explain to Anita what I needed her to hear and learn. But I had one last question to ask. "Anita, does your dad live around here?"

Again, the sadness, this time more quickly and much grayer. "No, I have never met him. My uncle used to tell me stories about him, the same stories my mama had told *tio* (uncle) of. I think he lives somewhere in the United States."

Not having any reason to wait any longer I slowly said, "Anita, I have something very important to tell you and it may sound a bit incredible, but please, listen with an open heart and an open mind."

I cleared my voice as her gaze upon me turned from sad to

concerned and then to serious. "Anita, I gave that ring that is around your neck to your mother many years ago when we were both young." Now shaking and with my voice trembling I continued. "I am your father. My real name was Rhet Austen and I had it changed just slightly to Rico Austin."

"No," was her quick and absolute response, then a sob with the word, "Papa," and then I was embraced by my daughter of nearly 20 years whom I had just met. After both of us had a tremendous cry of happiness and many hugs we decided it best to get out of the sun as the intense heat and some humidity had our tears intertwined with our beads of sweat.

We walked hand in hand back to the dirt parking lot and agreed to have dinner so each of us could share our lives with each other.

I went back to the Fiesta Hotel but made a stop at a dumpster placed between an old church and a beer *tienda* (store). I took the sundress I had found that morning and buried it deep under some garbage, being extra careful to make sure that no one had watched or seen me. I was going to start anew I vowed to myself, "I will not let this little mistake ruin my reunion with my new-found little girl."

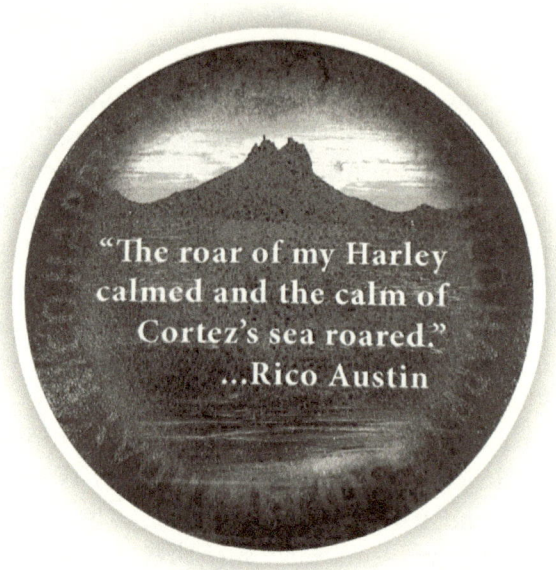

EPILOGUE

That night at dinner we talked, we laughed, and we cried. Our stories took hours and the Captain's Club restaurant accommodated us as we were the last to leave.

Anita shared that not long after her mother met me, she had been contacted by her brother (Anita's uncle) who had been living in Mexico after having crashed the Valentino's small airplane into one of the homes they provided for their fruit workers. One of the young Mexican men had died in the crash and Anita's Uncle Tony had but a few scratches. He had been drunk and should not have been flying the plane. Her grandfather, Tony's father, had been angry, but was a powerful man and would see to it that "things were taken care of."

Anita had told me that her mother had loved me very much and handed me the blue diary I knew so well, which Tony had given her on her *quinceaneras* (15th birthday party). We poured and sipped through it together, laughing and crying. Anita knew the dates and where to find all the fun and tragic stories of her mother and me.

My Bad Tequila

Tony had been extremely remorseful when he found out that the young immigrant farm worker had a wife and two children in Obregon, Sonora and went there to offer apologies and to provide for the family. After some time, he fell in love with the widow and her two children. He married her and remained in Mexico. He never spoke to his father again. He had also chosen not to have contact with his mother, but for different reasons. Tony had stayed in touch with Tina and had told her of his whereabouts in Mexico. She had contemplated going to see her brother many times, so when I had decided to go on Spring Break to Mexico in a town that was near where Tony lived, she decided to go as well. Tina had told me the last night I saw her that she was pregnant and was about to tell me about her brother coming to visit, but I had become angry, and she believed I did not want the child. Tina knew she could not go home pregnant, especially without the father wanting to make an honest woman of her. She knew Senator Valentino would demand she abort the child or be cast out from the family. Tina's mother was a good woman but weak when it came to family decisions and she would not cross the senator, even for her children. After our final tequila-laced fight Tina had called her brother and he had come and picked her up. Tina had written that she had seen me the next day; it was her in that pickup, with her brother and one of his friends. They were going to go to the hotel and gather her belongings, but decided against it and instead went back to Obregon. Tina and her brother had chosen not to call their mother as they were afraid their father would use his political power to make their decisions for them. The two Valentino children never saw or spoke to their parents again. Tony, his family, and Tina had all moved south to Puerto Vallarta to live for five years.

Tina had given birth to a beautiful baby girl and had named her Anita Valentino Austen. She moved back to San Carlos when Anita was five years of age as she wanted her daughter, our daughter, to know of its beauty and charm. She had started a local newspaper to keep herself occupied during the day after Anita had started her elementary education. The newspaper was printed in Spanish and in English for both locals and the visitors from the northern countries.

Anita and Tina lived in San Carlos, and eventually Tony moved his family from Puerto Vallarta to the same resort town where his sister and niece resided. Tina had become ill and was diagnosed with breast cancer when Anita was almost eleven years old. A year later Tina died, and Anita kept their small bungalow by the sea, but moved in with her uncle until she turned 18 and graduated from high school. Anita had earned her real estate license and met the developers of *Bahia Delfin*, who hired her to sell their upscale but affordable condos. She also worked part time at the newspaper with her Uncle Tony.

I told Anita of my travels and I shared with her my great marriage to her now stepmother Presley and of her being at the Oprah show that very August afternoon. Anita was extremely interested in hearing about Oprah Winfrey as she, too, adored her.

I chose to not tell her of the trial, or the time spent in prisons, both the walled Idaho penitentiary and the one in my mind of having thought that perhaps somehow, I had contributed to Tina's disappearance and death. I would tell her at another time, since my young daughter already had a great deal to digest without finding out her father had spent some of his life unjustly in a steel cage, wrongfully accused of her mother's disappearance and death. This conversation could wait for many days, perhaps months, or even years.

The next morning, we met again and drove back to *Bahia Delfin*, where I picked out a wonderful condo in the middle horseshoe near the swimming pool and with a perfect view of the ocean. It would also have an upstairs view of Tetakawi Mountain when the last brick of unit 532 was laid. Again, we had dinner, this time with Tony and his family. Tony was extremely friendly and gave me many hugs that night.

I left early the next day with a promise from Anita that she would visit for the entire months of December and January as she and the builders anticipated the condo complex being completely sold out by then.

As I left town, I picked up the morning paper Tina had

My Bad Tequila

founded and read the headline. "Woman from Hermosillo Last Seen Swimming with Tequila Drinking Gringo." I tossed the paper in the trash and sped out of town; north, for the border.

Rico Austin

THE END

Rico Austin

ABOUT THE AUTHOR

Born and raised in Southwestern Idaho, Rico is the oldest of five boys, growing up on a meager existence but in an area that was ripe for several adventures for him, his four younger brothers, and numerous cousins.

Rico grew up near farmland that produced potatoes, hay, hops, grain, and corn. There were several fruit orchards and vineyards in the Snake River Valley as well, due to the extraordinary fertile soil. A couple of years out of high school he moved to Boise and enrolled at Boise State University as a student and walk-on football player. However, he could not escape the allure of traveling the world and began writing and storing his experiences in hopes of someday becoming a novelist. He began by reading every chance he had. From contemporary novels to classical literature, Rico's love of storytelling was uncontrollable. He appeared occasionally at Boise's former Comedy Club as a standup comedian retelling his stories of growing up in a comedic fashion. Rico earned an Associate Degree in Marketing and Sales from BSU.

After a few years of low-level management positions Rico moved to Hawaii for a short time, surfing the waters of Kauai and enjoying the outdoors. He then moved to Southern California for less than a year before heading back to Idaho. In 1991 Rico moved to the Phoenix/Scottsdale area and continued his education, receiving a Bachelor of Business Administration in International Business at Grand Canyon University and received "Outstanding International Business Graduate of 1995." That same year he was also selected as "Mr. Future Business Executive" at the State Leadership Conference, which included all universities in the State of Arizona.

The summer before graduating Rico went to Vilnius,

My Bad Tequila

Lithuania and taught English (ESL). During the fall semester of his senior year at GCU, Rico attended Staffordshire University in England where he also started on the American Football Team for the Staffordshire Stallions. Rico finished his Masters, an MBA in International Management, at Thunderbird School of Global Management with a focus on the Latin American Region and the Spanish language. He did this while working full time as a feature writer and freelance journalist at the T-Bird school paper "DAS TOR." A few of his articles at "DAS TOR" were written in Spanish by Rico, specifically for the foreign students of Latin America.

Former Vice President Dan Quayle served as an "Invited Interim Professor by the Thunderbird School President for two semesters" and Rico was fortunate enough to be one of 16 students selected to attend his class. As a special note, Rico received an "A" from the VP for the two-credit elective class. Was it because of Rico's performance on studies or Quayle was afraid of what Mr. Austin might write in the paper?

Hollywood has even had an encounter with Rico. For those of you who watched Baywatch with the beautiful Pamela Anderson and David Hasselhoff, Mr. Rico Austin performed a cameo appearance in the episode "Day of the Dolphin" in 1997 where he played the role of a drug lord on a huge yacht with sexy chicks. He and his graduate classmates watched the episode when it aired in the "old clock tower hanger" together in the TV lounge. He was invited back for another episode by Producer and Casting Director Susie Glickman but had to decline due to a conflict with finals at Thunderbird. Rico chose education over stardom, when questioned why, he responded, "No one can ever take your education away, everything else can come and go and, most likely will." Rico also acted in a commercial for the local market in Boise, ID as a construction worker in "That Old House" sponsored by BMC West.

Rico is an avid fisherman and has traveled far and wide to cast his line into many waters, including streams, lakes, ponds, rivers, seas, and oceans. He has worked for a few international companies as both a sales manager and a marketing manager. In his spare time he has worked as a land developer and was a licensed realtor in Arizona.

Rico now is happily married to a graphic artist from Minnesota who works for a prominent company. They make their home in the "Land of the Sun": Scottsdale, Arizona. He and his wife Connie enjoy snorkeling, hiking, hanging by their swimming pool, and traveling to the beaches of Mexico while sipping on a cold cerveza or margarita blended with Rico's favorite TEQUILA which just so happens to be his own - BAJARRIBA.

Rico put an Arizona LLC together during Covid called Tres Cabo Amigos, LLC which was founded in October 2020. Together with two friends / partners he had met in Cabo San Lucas many years before while on a book signing tour. Both Jay and Miguel each had bars in Cabo, they later moved to Arizona and the three of them co-founded the Tequila brand BAJARRIBA of which Rico is the managing partner and obtained his Doctorates Degree in Tequila, earning his PhD in June 2016 from none other than Mr. Julio Bermejo, one of the most knowledgeable human beings of all things Tequila and the man who concocted the world famous 'Tommy's Margarita' in San Francisco. After earning his Doctorate Degree in Tequila, Rico stated, "I wasn't drinking, I was studying!'

Rico's wife Connie designed the bottle from Miguel's idea and the upside-down BAJA Peninsula shaped bottle won "Bottle / Packaging of the Year" in December of 2022 by Tequila Aficionado, the same month they launched their products in the states of Arizona and California. In 2023, they added the Las Vegas, Nevada market.

Rico and his tequila BAJARRIBA were on the cover of

My Bad Tequila

Tequila Aficionado for a record three times. Never before had a brand been on the cover more than once in a calendar year and BAJARRIBA and Rico graced the cover in April, a Special "Cinco de Mayo" issue in May and again in the December 2023 issue with Good Santa / Bad Santa. Rico was cast as "Bad Santa!" (www.Bajarriba.com)

Rico Austin first began writing seriously as a seventh grader at age 13. He was chosen as a reporter for the "Eager Beaver 4-H Club" in Marsing, Idaho and started submitting weekly articles to the local newspaper. Rico then was chosen as a reporter for the local FFA chapter during his freshman and sophomore year and continued to expand his writing ability. As a freshman Rico took third place in the Marsing High School essay contest titled, "American Beef Farmers." He later would write a few short stories for Reader's Digest and become a professional freelance and feature writer for DAS TOR newspaper at Thunderbird, The American Graduate School of Global Management from 1996 to 1998. Rico also won the first and only writing essay at DAS TOR in March 1997. The essay asked contestants to propose ways for Thunderbird to be improved. Rico used his humor, knowledge of several countries that he had traveled to, and innovation to secure the winning essay. One of his most serious assignments and pieces of journalism was reporting on the Winterim class 97 "US Foreign Economic Policy" in Washington, DC including the opening of the 105th Congress the Inauguration of the President of the United States, Mr. Bill Clinton.

Favorite movie: "Gone With the and Wind" & the new movie "Hangover" for a comedy. His favorite books are: John Steinbeck's "East of Eden" Ernest Hemingway's "The Old Man and the Sea" J.R.R. Tolkien's "The Hobbit" Rico's first novel, "MY BAD TEQUILA" was published in September 2010. The hit single song "My Bad Tequila" was co-written by Rico and Elly Garrison, who also sings and performs the song with her band QuarterDeck, and can be found on iTunes, Yahoo Music, and Amazon Music. www.QuarterDeckCountry.com

REVIEWS

"I finished the book....unbelievable. One of the best endings that I have read. I like the way you write...and look back at your life, etcetera. I will definitely recommend to my friends both in US and Mexico to buy the book.! *Muy bueno*. Also, I downloaded the song *My Bad Tequila* from iTunes...I like it, nice job from you and Quarterdeck!" —*Mike Gregory, Scottsdale, Arizona*

"Rico Austin's book *My Bad Tequila* is a great ride. I never know what crazy thing is going to happen next. I love the wit and honesty that it is written with. I feel as if I am right there with the characters, experiencing their crazy Mexican vacation. Rico's writing style is fresh and real. I love it! Very Funny!" — *Crystal Lockwood, Award Winning Sculptress, San Francisco Bay, California (http://www.crystallockwood.com)*

"LOVED the book! Had a hard time putting it down. You made everything so vivid. At one point thought I was having a Dean Koontz experience. Going to Amazon right now to order a copy for my cousin."—*Karen B., who purchased the novel during a book signing event at Qwest Arena in Boise, Idaho*

"Rico, I loved your book! Fascinating story! I finished it in a couple days because it was a fun read. I liked having a little Spanish refresher, too. Of course, being familiar with San Carlos made your book even more special! We have told several of our friends & family who know San Carlos about your book. Even my doctor saw me reading it in her office and asked about it. Since she loves San Carlos and has been to Club Med, she is going to buy it! See you in SC and MAYBE have some tequila :)"—*Ms. Nancy G., San Carlos, Sonora, Mexico*

"I had just finished Mr. Rico's novel at 3:30 this morning. The quasi-auto biography reminded me of Kurt Vonnegut's quasi-auto biography 'Time Quake.' There are three major differences in the two novels. 1. Rico's book was well written 2. Rico's book had a point 3. Rico's book was a good read. I am looking forward to his next novel."
—*Randy Shippy, Middleton, Idaho*

"Rico's love of storytelling is infectious" said one loyal reader and friend at a recent party, "Once you read one, you have to read all of his short stories."—*Steven Boyce, Hollywood actor, stuntman, Harley rider, Long Beach, California*

LEARN MORE

Join our Fan Page on Face Book for *Amigas* & *Amigos* at:
"Official My Bad Tequila Fan Page"

Check out MY BAD TEQUILA's BLOG:
http://blog.mybadtequila.com

Keep up with the latest MY BAD TEQUILA news:
http://www.mybadtequila.com

Join Rico on Facebook
https://www.facebook.com/rico.austin/

https://www.facebook.com/BajarribaTequila/

https://www.instagram.com/bajarribatequila/

Check out MY BAD TEQUILA BLOG:
http://blog.mybadtequila.com

My Bad Tequila

Rico Austin

Rico has always had a dream of owning his own tequila brand and finally in October 2020 that dream began to take shape as he shared his vision with two Amigos - Jay and Mike of whom he had met in Cabo San Lucas, Mexico years earlier who have since moved to the Land of the Sun in AZ. Rico formed the Tres Cabo Amigos, LLC and with the help of his wife Connie and Marinette, it is a 51% women owned company with Rico as Managing Partner and Spokesperson.

Bajarriba® Tequila is 100% Blue Weber Agave additive free with NO artificial taste, smell or coloring. Its ingredients are agave, water and yeast - nothing else! The distillery is 3rd generation, founded 1937 in the highlands of Atotonilco, Jalisco MX at elevation 7000 feet using Old World time tested, cooking method with pure, deep well water, copper/stainless steel pots and slow roasting in "hornos" (brick ovens) for ultimate flavor. The agaves are fully matured at an average of eight years, grown in rich fertile volcanic soil of the highlands.

Bajarriba and other great tequilas being distilled at NOM 1107 are considered by many connoisseurs, enthusiasts and most tequila drinkers to be some of the finest tasting tequilas in the world.

Bajarriba was awarded by Tequila Aficionado Media and Magazine the Platinum Award/1st place "Bottle of the Year/Packaging" and "Brand of Promise" finalist for both Plata & Reposado Expressions in December 2022.

Bajarriba has been on the cover of Tequila Aficionado a record three times in less than one calender year. No other brand has ever been on the cover more than once in a year. Bajarriba was on the cover of April 2023 issue and Special Edition "Cinco de Mayo" 2023 issue and concluded with the December 2023 issue, (all pictured on left).

My Bad Tequila

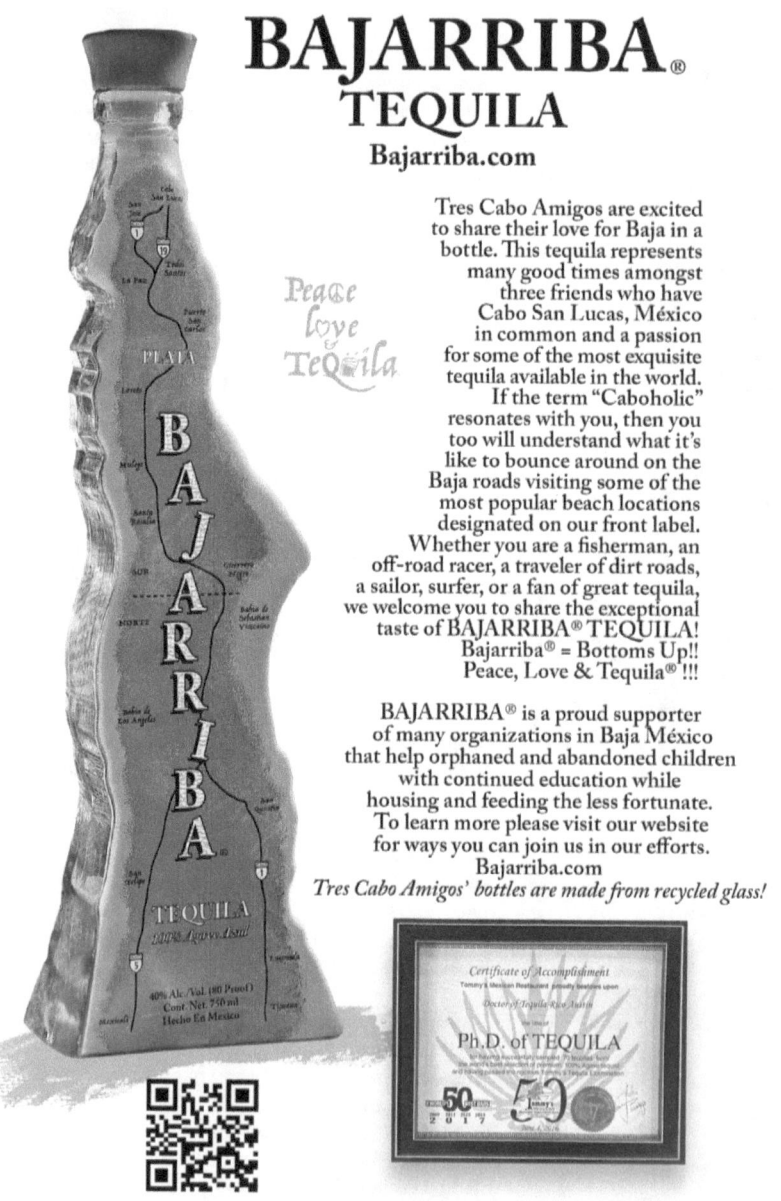

www.ingramcontent.com/pod-product-compliance
Lightning Source LLC
LaVergne TN
LVHW092013090526
838202LV00030B/2639/J